The Human Search Engine™ Workbook: A Serious Jobseekers Guide

Copyright© 2014 by Career Research Group

ISBN 978-0-692-35148-2

Printed in the USA by Bouwer Printing

DEDICATION

No project of this magnitude is completed without the help of others. I want to extend a heartfelt thanks to the thousands of people who trusted me and the HSE process with helping them find their path towards a more rewarding career.

To Doug Tiedt and Kelli Richards at UW Madison who gave me the first opportunity to teach the HSE process as curriculum at a major college level. This never happens without your belief in my work. Go Badgers!

To Dr. Susan May, President of Fox Valley Technical College who gave me the opportunity to work with hundreds of people with the creation of the Job Seekers Network at FVTC. You believed in me first…

And to my Jennifer who has stayed by my side through the joys and sorrows of bringing this to life. Your belief kept me going when times got tough…you are my soul mate, my light and my love…we are an unbeatable team.

Table of Contents

FORWARD

From Shawano, Wisconsin, to the White House

After more than a decade of teaching career search, I have met many amazing people and seen incredible transformations from individuals who embrace the Human Search Engine Process. These success stories are sometimes even hard to believe. While writing this book, I smiled at myself because as I have told others, "The stories are so incredible that I'm going to need to publish it under fiction." Among all of these stories, one sticks out more than the rest: the story of Steve G.

I first met Steve as a client after I had taught career search for a couple of years. He came to our initial meeting uncertain and afraid. While that is not entirely unusual for job search clients, there was something different here—I recognized him.

Steve had spent the majority of his working life in the emergency management field, and he was good at it. His work was all about preparing for and responding to emergency situations like tornados, floods, mass chemical spills and other natural and man-made disasters. His job was one that you and I spend very little time thinking about—until we need it.

One area of his expertise was in managing the situation and resources that come into play immediately after a disaster strikes. His ability to prepare for disasters that had not yet occurred was equally important, but he was the person in the headlines when an incident occurred. If you have ever thought, "Wow, somebody should do something about that horrible disaster," then Steve was the person you were referring to.

I recognized his name from some 7 or 8 years earlier. There had been a train derailment near Weyauwega, a small city in east central Wisconsin. The train cars that derailed were filled with toxic chemicals. It was all over the news, and citizens of Weyauwega and surrounding communities had to completely evacuate the area as it was quarantined for a massive clean-up effort.

Steve was a member of the Incident Commander Team regarding the response to this tragedy. He was recognized later as having done an incredible job organizing and executing the response and recovery efforts as part of the team. His work on behalf of hundreds of other responders was acknowledged across the state.

The subsequent years after this incident had not been kind to Steve's career. Through a series of budget cuts and a de-emphasizing of emergency management at various government levels, his position had been reduced over and over again. When Steve finally walked into my office he was barely hanging onto a 20 hour-a-week job in the smaller community of Shawano, Wisconsin. Even worse, that position was in danger of being reduced even further and perhaps eliminated altogether. The term Steve used in our first meeting was that he had gone from the "penthouse to the outhouse." He was scared, humbled and lost in his search.

As with every other client, I started to walk him through my process (That's what is cool about HSE being a process. Whether the client is an astronaut or a circus clown, the process remains the same. Whatever your area of expertise is in, the process is the answer… and that's why it can work for anyone.). We walked through achievements and skills, objectives and Networking Briefs. Through the process I could see that

Steve's confidence was returning. He began to realize that his skills and abilities hadn't changed; it was just that the right people weren't seeing him that way at the moment.

We started our search by identifying people who had been critical to Steve's success with the emergency management work he did so successfully in the past (his ABC List). Then we determined that his work with a few of the local Native American tribes turned out to be some of his most successful and enjoyable endeavors. He made a list of people with whom he had conversed during these tribal experiences. It was comprised of contacts that had a high level of confidence in him. He proceeded to set up Networking Meetings and Informational Interviews with them.

To Steve's great surprise, these people were very WILLING to help him with his search because they remembered him for the great work he had done for them in the past. While his opinion of himself had faded, these people treated him as an invaluable resource. In a short period of time (two or maybe three connections later), he was asked to do some part-time emergency planning for one of the local tribes. He was thrilled! Someone thought he was good enough again!

Now convinced in the power of the process, Steve didn't stop. During his part-time work he was coming into contact with dozens of people who lived in the world of emergency management. He was making connections and building relationships. His Informational Interviews with these people centered on where his skill set might be most valued. It wasn't long before his reputation spread throughout the Native American community. Eventually a number of tribes created a full-time position through a Federal grant. That's right… a position was created for him through the process. He wasn't done yet…

Steve continued to network (the right way as taught by the process) in the emergency management sector not knowing he would need it again. Once again he found himself facing the same dilemma. The new position was being eliminated and Steve would be jobless in a few months. He took action this time by using the network he built and immediately sent notifications to people within this circle of diverse individuals.

It was not long before one of his connections asked Steve if he would like to come and work for FEMA (Federal Emergency Management Agency) to help with the flooding from hurricane Katrina in New Orleans. Steve jumped at the opportunity. From part-time in Shawano to a full-time contractor with FEMA in less than a year and a half, but that's not where the story ends.

I am proud to say that through a series of promotions, Steve became a manager in the FEMA organization and was transferred to Washington, D.C. After about five years of diligent work, he has become one of the go-to-individuals in Washington in his area of expertise. In 2011, he was named the Director of Tribal Affairs for the Department of Homeland Security. That's right, the same guy who was seen by others as barely good enough to hang onto a part-time job in a town of 10,000 in east central Wisconsin now attends briefings in the White House. Not bad, huh?

I met with Steve while writing this book to ask his permission to include his story. Amazingly (or maybe not so), he was the exact same humble guy that I had met years earlier. In fact, that's one of the secrets to his success. ***Be humble, be sincere and ask for help***, I want you to remember these three concepts throughout this entire book. Over lunch in a crab shack in Annapolis, Maryland, he gave his consent to be in the book. With a smile he said, "Go ahead and put me in the book, but nobody's ever going to believe it."

INTRODUCTION

Job seekers are being held captive to a hiring process that is broken. The strategy of sending out resumes to complete strangers to try and capture their attention is tantamount to begging for a job. Placing a job ad online and scanning through hundreds or thousands of resumes in hopes to find the perfect employee is just as wasteful. Utilizing current job search methods means a job seeker can only apply for jobs that are advertised…and then has to mold themselves into someone who fits it. As I will show you, this kind of activity excludes job seekers from being considered for the more than 75% of all jobs that are never advertised.

…But what if there was another way?

The purpose of this book is to teach an entirely different way to find your next job. You will be guided through a process that gives you control over your search at all times. Instead of a job search, it's a logical and controllable research project based on **Definition, Research and Marketing**…the same methods that Fortune 500 companies have been using for decades to develop and market new products.

I have successfully trained thousands of job seekers how to use the process in this book, which I refer to as the Human Search Engine (HSE) Process – and by "successfully" I mean they are now employed. This process is logical, sequential and terminal – if you do the work you WILL land a job. The basic precepts of proactive job search, which HSE is built on, have been used by high level executives for many years…unfortunately the way to perform such a search has never been standardized or accessible to everyone.

Executing this process is hard work. This is not an "annoy-everyone-you-meet", "get-hired-quick" scheme. Each assignment must be completed in its entirety before moving on to the next task. Like almost everything else in life, you will get out of it what you put into it…but you will also find this a fascinating journey. It is a journey that is designed to lift you up, build your confidence and prepare you to present yourself in the best possible way to the job market in your area. You will also learn that hiring managers are hoping to find their next great employee in this exact way. People who use the HSE Process simplify the hiring process, avoid HR and get directly to the decision makers in an organization.

The most important part of the process is that *you* will be in control of your search every step of the way. You will control your assignment outputs, your message, the problems you hope to solve and the organizations you choose to approach. You will control who you meet with and what to do with the information you learn from your conversations. You will ultimately control where you go to work. That's what you really want after all, isn't it?

Proactive job search is now your job….so let's get to work!

CHAPTER 1: CHANGE YOUR JOB SEARCH MINDSET

How you find everything of value in your life

If you think about how people look for a job, it is different than the way they look for anything else. Typically, job seekers look for open jobs that are posted by people they don't know, in order to go to work for organizations that they may have never heard of. Then, if there are no jobs posted that they can "creatively" make themselves look qualified for, there is nothing they can do until tomorrow's job postings come out. Is that how people look for anything else in their life?

How would you buy a new house? Would you ever do it in the same way that most people look for a job? It would look something like this:

- ✓ Drive down random streets
- ✓ Make an offer on first house you see for sale
- ✓ Change your lifestyle to fit the house you just bought

Of course you wouldn't do that! How *would* you buy a house? Surely a $200,000 decision is too important to make without some criteria, right?

First you would DEFINE what you were looking for. Three or four bedrooms? What city must it be in? What price range fits your budget? What school district should it be in? Traditional ranch or modern craftsman style? In the city or in the country? For a decision this big you would NEVER move forward without first DEFINING what the right house looks like.

After DEFINING what you are looking for you would RESEARCH the houses in the area that fit your criteria. What size home are you able to afford on your budget? What are the best school districts in the area? What are the crime rates for the cities you are considering? Which neighborhoods best suit your needs? Is mass transit available? What are property taxes going to be? For the most part, this information could be obtained by talking with people who live in the area.

The last step in purchasing your new home would be to match your needs to people who are MARKETING homes that fit them. You would talk to local experts who buy and sell houses (realtors) to get advice, guidance and feedback on where to find the right home. You might drive through neighborhoods that match your criteria and find homes that are for sale. You could even talk to people who own homes like you want to find or get referred to other people who have similar homes for sale.

Purchasing a home is a really big decision and you would never make that kind of decision without doing your homework. So why would you look for a job any other way?

More importantly, employers do not want to spend 100 hours in a hiring selection process if they don't have to. They would love to have the new employee they are looking for appear in front of them without having to spend a ton of time doing it.

> ## *Change your job search mindset.*

Key elements to the Human Search Engine (HSE) Process

A common theme that dominates my first meeting with any job seeker nters around fundamentally changing their attitude about how they should present themselves during their job search. In layman's terms, they need to "unlearn" everything they THINK they know about job search. The first thing we discuss is how they will present themselves to the world during the process.

Traditional job search methods teach people that the best way to present themselves during their job search is to puff out their chest and confidently mesmerize the people they are meeting with a half dozen or so stories about how great they are and how they have "almost single-handedly changed the fortunes" of an organization. The goal (so you have been told) is to impress people so much during your interaction that they will spontaneously throw their arms around you and declare, "I can't believe we have finally found you! Can you start on Monday for $90,000 a year with four weeks of vacation and stock options?" That is a beautiful dream, but that's all it is. I often refer to this as the "fairy tale ending" to your job search. You have seen it in movies, read about it in magazines and hope with all your heart that this is how your job search will end. The problem is, it just isn't true.

How has that worked for you so far?

The fact is, you know better. You have never created a meaningful relationship in your life that way, but somehow now it's going to work because some internet job blog told you it would? Isn't it more likely that you will create this new networking or job relationship the same way that you have created every other meaningful relationship in your life? Have you ever created a new relationship by impressing people with your skills, talents and abilities the first time the two of you met? Not likely.

Let's be clear, there will be plenty of time during the interview phase of your job search where telling your achievement stories will be valuable. As a matter of fact, you will write out achievement narratives as part of the HSE Process for use at the right time. This point in the process is about asking for and garnering support. You will be asking people who are WILLING to help you find people that are ABLE to help you, but not in the way you'd expect. First I'll introduce you to the most important precursor to the process.

> ## *Be humble, be sincere, and ask for help.*

Be humble - Try to envision the last person you met who was really obnoxious. There was no way the two of you were going to strike up a friendship of any type. What was it about them? Were they opinionated? Did they work too hard to impress you with how wealthy or athletic they were? Did they let you get a word in edgewise? My guess is that you tuned out the first minute of your conversation because they were not humble.

While people are drawn to confidence, they run screaming from bravado. if the intent is to ask people to assist you in your search, going over the top to tell them how great you are will likely alienate them or worse yet have them ask themselves, "If they are so great, what do they need my help for?"

When was the last time that you turned your back on a truly humble or genuine person? Now ask yourself when was the last time you turned away from someone who was too full of themselves?

Be sincere - I'm not sure which group of people you would identify as least sincere, but I'm guessing politicians and used car dealers would rank right up there. You can smell insincerity a mile away. As George Burns once quipped, "Once you can fake sincerity, you've got it made." Don't fake sincerity, be sincere. Most people have a pretty good BS detector.

The picture of an insincere used car dealer telling a gullible car buyer they will get this deal "today only because I like your face" is part of our lexicon. Never try to fool anyone with insincerity because it's akin to lying and people run from it.
During this process you are going to ask people for "advice, guidance and feedback" on your search. No back door resume drops, no getting in front of important people to ask for advice and then try turning it into a job interview. People in the position to hire other people have a common trait. They read people well. That's how they got into that position. Insincerity stinks like rotten fish; it's easy to spot and almost impossible to overcome.

The HSE Process is the kind of job search process that has been used by upper level management-type people for decades. They would never think of doing their search any other way. The people you are about to network with know exactly how it works. They have very likely done a similar search in their lives and are ready to help you, but only if you follow the rules.

Ask for help - Many psychological studies have identified the word "help" as one of the words most likely to get people to listen and to spur them to action. A broken down car on the side of the road with its hood up is a universal request for help. Complete strangers stop their journey to their house at the sight of an open hood. Why?

Even the most self-absorbed person is hard wired to respond to a request for help. Whether they act on the request for help is another matter, but they listen. Fundraising telemarketers appeal to strangers who have never seen their face to "help" them fund their cause. The word "help" screamed out of the darkness draws well-meaning strangers to the site to see how they can be of assistance. People respond to requests for help, but only if the request is reasonable, and they can relate to it.

Considering that you will not be asking strangers for help, but asking people already WILLING to help, how do you think they will respond? The request for help needs to be reasonable and they must be able to relate to it. Asking someone for help finding a job is not a reasonable request because it is not well defined, creates a lot of work for them and drops your unemployment problem in their lap. That's not networking, that's begging. **It's the difference between asking someone for advice on the best pizza in town or asking them to drive you to the restaurant and buy the pizza for you.**

You have asked for help many times in your life. If the request was reasonable and people could relate to it, they helped you. How could asking for help with your job search be any different? That's the important thing about the HSE Process. To judge whether this theory is true or not, just compare it with the experiences in your own life.

Proactive vs. reactive job search.

Be humble, be sincere and ask for help. It beats the heck out of the "try and impress complete strangers strategy," doesn't it?

The problem with traditional job search methods is that the job seeker has been taught that there is nothing they can do to go after a new position until a position is posted. This is fundamentally false.

There are dozens of studies completed over several decades that indicate **65-85% of all jobs are never advertised to the public.** That's right, while you are waiting for job ads to be posted, other people are landing positions that will never be made public.

In fact, what will frustrate you most is that in many cases employers only post their open positions as a last resort after exhausting all other forms of recruiting…and it gets worse. If a company has the best job with the best pay, benefits and working conditions, why would they EVER need to advertise that job? They can easily fill that job just by a little word of mouth advertising…no need to ever make the opening public.

When summing up how the HSE Process works, I often tell job seekers they are going to" put a ham sandwich in front of a hungry person and let them decide if they want to eat it. If they aren't hungry simply ask them to refer you to other hungry people." Simple, right? Isn't that what recruiters do? But to do so requires you to determine what type of ham sandwich to make (Definition), how to present it and where the hungry people who eat ham sandwiches go for lunch (Research) and then go to the right place with the right sandwich and place it front of those hungry souls (Marketing).

Why do people hire other people?

So you have a choice: Sit back and hope that the job of your dreams falls out of the sky and into your lap, or implement a logical and strategic plan you have used many times already in your life to find important things. Which option do you choose?

This one idea will likely change your view of hiring from this point forward:

"People hire other people to solve their problems, make their life easier and get them closer to their next goal or bonus."

People don't get hired just because there is a job opening; they get hired because they create more value for the company than they are getting paid. That's it. Everything else is fluff. When you begin to tell your story in terms of creating value for an organization, you are halfway home.

What exactly does that mean? It means that finding your next employer comes down to two questions:

First know yourself

1.   **What problems are you uniquely able to solve?**

2.   **Who has those problems?**

That's it. So the examples you will use on your resume and cover letter had better answer those questions. Your answers in interviews had better answer those questions. Your research to find companies to approach had better answer those questions.

Your job search should start with the question, "Who am I?" Please note the question isn't about what you have done or who you have done it for. Often when people are asked who they are, they respond by saying what they do. If you are unemployed, that's not going to work very well. The question really is, "Who are you when nobody is around? On weekends? With friends?"

A fundamental problem among job seekers is they think they need to change who they are to fit into a job. How silly is that? They see a job ad and then decide if they can mold themselves into what the employer is looking for. Does that make any sense? (As in the earlier example of purchasing a home and then fitting your lifestyle into it – it's backwards).

Two reasons job seekers do this:

1. **They have been taught to do job search that way.**

2. **They are not sure that who they really are is good enough to get a great job.**

The HSE Process is all about changing the way that you perform your job search in order to find a job that really allows you to be you. Changing who you are to go to work is a ticking time bomb that has derailed thousands of careers. Misalignment with the job and a person's personality is the number one reason that I have seen people fail to be successful in their career. Let's start fixing that now.

CHAPTER 2: THE FUNDAMENTAL PROBLEMS OF JOB SEARCH

Jobseekers and employers can't find each other

One day after teaching an HSE job search class, I was scheduled to deliver a short address to fifteen HR people and hiring managers from mid- to large-size companies. I sat at one of the tables and greeted attendees. Some of the guests had vaguely heard about the job search program I was teaching and started asking me questions. The rest of the table small quickly became involved in the topic of searching for talented new employees.

"Where is all the talent out there, Chris?" one asked. The faces of almost all of the company reps turned to me with looks of frustration. The same person continued, "We have been advertising for an operations manager with specific skills for nearly three months now, and the resumes we have received don't fit at all. It's like the applicants aren't reading the ad and just apply using generic resumes and cover letters, regardless of if they actually qualify to do the job," he concluded.

There was implied agreement from at least half of the table that this appeared to be a real problem for them as well. I wanted to stand on my chair and yell, "The talented people who you are looking for are just down the hall in my job search class!" I usually jump at these opportunities to provide helpful information, but I didn't. I was so taken by what I just heard that I froze.

A few minutes later something hit me: **The biggest problem in job search is that employers and jobseekers can't find each other.** Take a moment to digest that…the only real reason people stay unemployed is that the organization that needs them as their next great employee can't find them. The HSE Process shows you how to become much easier for the organizations that are looking for you to find -- and then how to have a compelling story to share once they find you (or you find them).

The two biggest problems every job seeker faces

⇒ *Nobody knows you exist*

⇒ *You are unaware of 85% of organizations that are out there*

> *Problem#1:*
> *Nobody*
> *knows you*
> *exist*

Conversations with job seekers often start with them saying: "Anybody who knows me knows what a good (manager, accountant or salesperson) I am." Think about that statement for a second…What is wrong with it in terms of a job search? The person who has the problems you are uniquely qualified to solve doesn't know you. If they did they would already be talking to you. For every job seeker, one of two things has to be true: **Either the person or organization that needs you can't find you, or nobody needs you** (After working with thousands of job seekers, I've never found the second part to be true). People don't understand that organizations are constantly looking for talent, but they don't know where or how to find it. Your job during this process is to make you easier to find for the people that need you. Remember the ham sandwich example?

The problem of being unknown to the people who need you is the most important problem to solve during your search. Solve this problem and you will find opportunities. Solve this problem and you will be sitting in front of people who need you or they will refer you to someone that does.

As a final thought about not being known by most of the people in your community, I'll share my own experience on the topic.

Example: Oktoberfest

I have lived my entire life in a community of about 250,000 people. My job is to speak to or teach thousands of people each year. That work requires me to be on TV, radio and in the newspaper…My job is to be known.

Each year this community holds an Oktoberfest where 90,000 people congregate along a one mile stretch of street for a huge celebration. Each year I walk through that enormous crowd for two hours and count the people I run into who I know. I have yet to know more than 20 people there. The conclusion is clear: If people don't know someone whose job it is to be in the public eye, what are the chances that people know you? People can't hire you until they know you exist. And they don't know you exist right now, so let's change that.

> **Problem#2:**
> **You are**
> **unaware of**
> **85% of jobs**

In any given community there are certain organizations everyone has heard of. When these companies advertise job openings, hundreds of people apply because everyone knows of the company. In that same community though, there are literally hundreds, if not thousands, of organizations that are fine places to work, offer good pay and benefits and present real job opportunities. Because these organizations rarely make the news, most people in the community are completely unaware of their existence and therefor never consider them as places to work. This is a big mistake.

Back in my community, databases show that there are about 32,000 organizations within a thirty mile radius. Most job seekers couldn't name more than 100 of them. Are you beginning to see the problem?

You can't go to work for an organization you don't know exists.

Job seekers must identify these lesser known organizations as places that have problems that they are uniquely able to solve, so they can be "standing in a line of one" in the interview process. Remember, the larger the company, the more layers of HR you need to penetrate just to talk to a real live person. Interviewing at a small company (which still provides great pay, opportunities and challenges) means you do not have seven layers of HR to get through…or more importantly that you may be one just a few people who are aware of and pursuing that opportunity. My advice is not to stand in a line of 100 applying to a company that everyone has heard of. Instead, identify lesser known organizations and you could be the only one in line for that job. Later in the book I'll show you how to research companies other job seekers have overlooked. For now, there is research to be done and diamonds to be uncovered.

Simply being qualified is not enough. The next concept you must understand is that in my experience **the number one reason people stay unemployed is that there is nothing unique about them.**

Think about hiring from "the other side of the desk," from the view of the person screening resumes or the HR manager deciding who they should bring in for an interview. They put an ad online or in the newspaper that contains certain job requirements and qualifications. Then what happens? They are overwhelmed by 100's of resumes from strangers all stating that they can "turn stones into gold, water into wine and tiptoe across the lake on the way to work every day."

> *Being unique means being employed*

This makes the initial screening process is simple. It starts by eliminating the people that don't fit the qualifications or experience requirements. That narrows the field down to about twenty genuinely qualified applicants. To get from twenty candidates down to the four that will be interviewed is a little more complicated. This is where your ability to create uniqueness in your message will make you stand out from the rest. If you are not unique in the message you send, you end up looking like everyone else in that pile of twenty candidates. **Your message needs to not only indicate that you are qualified, but that you bring something to the conversation that is different than what the other candidates bring.** If it doesn't, how can they choose you from the pile?

The goal in this part of the HSE Process is to create a message that is so unique and so compelling that your resume and networking brief (more on that later) jump out of the pile! So as you think about your job search, always keep in mind that being qualified doesn't get you hired. What gets you hired is being a qualified candidate who presents themselves in a way that is impossible to overlook.

Is your passion for the work what will make you unique? If so, how will you tell that story? Is it a unique set of experiences that will set you apart? Have you solved a problem that others in your industry have struggled to figure out? Has your work in the past created results that are far and away greater than that of the other people in your line of work? What is it that will catch their attention?

Think for a moment about all of the restaurants that have come and gone in the city where you live. Most likely the ones that failed had perfectly good food and service. They likely had pricing that put them on par with other competing places to eat…but there was likely nothing unique about them that made people think of them when it came time to find a place to eat. **I'm guessing the restaurants that do really well where you live are known for something.**

Whether it is an amazing view or a specialized menu, there is a reason that people keep going back. A restaurant that advertises average food at average prices with an average view for average people goes out of business **not because they are not qualified to feed you but because there is nothing to make you remember them or choose them over all of the other places to eat.**

I believe that **you have to become interesting before you can become important.** If I can't find you in the pile of qualified candidates you have made it impossible for me to hire you. The HSE Process is about a new way to get your message in front of hiring managers. Let's make sure that once you get the message in front of them they are so moved they cannot wait to meet you.

CHAPTER 3: DEFINITION, RESEARCH AND MARKETING DEFINITIONS

Definition, Research, and Marketing – the instructional content of HSE

It is important to point out that the process you are about to undertake is not new nor is it unproven…quite the contrary. As I mentioned before, it mimics the process that virtually every billion dollar, international organization uses to create and market new products. For example, is it coincidence that football games are filled with commercials for products that are primarily focused on 30-55 year old men (luxury cars, alcoholic beverages or health/fitness products)…no accident at all. Companies **define** the problems and interests that group of men have, they **research** what products they are competing against and then they **market** the products by advertising them where people who need or value them are likely to be watching. The use of this process is around you every day. And everyone knows…IT WORKS!

Definition

Before a product can be marketed to anyone, the first step is to define what this product or service *is and is not*. These are the questions that have to be answered (write them down and keep them handy as you start your HSE Process to put clear definition around what is being sold or marketed. In this case, that's YOU!).

✓ **What does your product or service do?**

✓ **What does it look like?**

✓ **What problems does it solve?**

✓ **Is there anything else like it?**

✓ **What are its benefits and features that will appeal to customers?**

Most importantly, can you define this product or service in a way that is easy to understand to the general public? If you make the mistake of over-defining in very technical terms, then the ability to market a product, service or even ourselves to the general public becomes ineffective.

Research

After you have clearly defined 'what' you will be promoting to the marketplace, the next step is to do research on it and the market(s) it is to be sold into. To put this concept into a tangible, sequential context, consider these questions:

✓ **What problems exist that people need to solve?**

✓ **Who has these problems and why?**

✓ **Why can't they solve those problems with their current or other tried resources?**

✓ What is the cost in time and money, in addition to negative effects, if the problems are not solved or if an opportunity is not seized?

✓ What are people willing to pay for a solution to the problems?

✓ Does a solution provide opportunities in other, less obvious markets as well?

Marketing

Now that you have a product or a service that is well defined and you are convinced that people need it, how do you make people aware of its availability? Consider these marketing ideas:

✓ What advertising channels exist?

✓ Who are the industry experts who can evaluate the value of the product or service?

✓ How do you create word-of-mouth advertising to promote it?

✓ How do you help people decide that they need it instead of pushing this thing on them?

✓ Who is willing to help promote this once they know its value?

✓ What industry specific words, phrases or concepts need to be part of the marketing plan?

✓ Whose endorsement or recommendation do we need?

The three-category process that I have just outlined goes on in offices around the world every day. Whether someone is creating a new sports drink, an electronic gadget or promoting a candidate for public office, the process is always the same. It's fair to think that if this process works for billion dollar, multi-national corporations, it's good enough for you. I am not prescribing a magic pill—just a proven method that goes on around you every day in every part of your life.

CHAPTER 4: BEGINNING STEPS TO THE HSE JOB SEARCH PROCESS

DEFINITION

As a job seeker, the first question you should answer is, "What is really important to me?" If you can align what is important to you with the work that you do for a living then you "will never work a day in your life." Figuring out your personality type will assist you in answering this question, and thankfully there are several tools that can help you figure it out.

Search online using the phrase "free personality test". You will find several tests of about 40 questions to answer about your preferences.

Answer the questions based on your preferences when you are relaxed and not stressed (on vacation, for example). The result will be some personality type that you can research online. There will be profiles and descriptions about your personality type and you will know if you got it right when you read this description. You should read it and say, "How could anyone know that about me? This sounds exactly like me!"

People often laugh when reading the descriptions because they are so accurate. Share your personality profile with your significant other and ask them if it sounds like you when you are on vacation or on the weekends. That is the key.

While you are researching your particular profile, pay attention to things that are important to your personality type, and what makes that type happy. Also note what types of jobs people like you flourish in. All of this will be helpful in creating the profile of what you are looking for in your next position.

> *Define Yourself: Do not continue with the HSE Process until you have done some personality research for yourself. Knowing yourself first is the very foundation of the Process. What could be more important than that?*

Identify your achievements

In detail, write 7-10 **work, school or life** achievements that you are most proud of or brought the most value to your organization. Focus on achievements where you played an integral role in making them happen. This is no time for modesty. Your past achievements are the best indication that a future employer has on how you can solve problems, make life easier, and get closer to attaining goals. Turn each achievement into a <u>short</u> story- about one legal-size page long. Do it in a way so a person who was not there during that event can understand the situation by putting him or herself in the same setting. We will refer to these as <u>ACV</u> **(Ability to Create Value)** narratives.

Focus on three important areas:

- ✓ **What did you do?**
- ✓ **How did you do it?**
- ✓ **What was the result?**

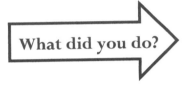

Make sure to give the reader (someone other than you) a good feel for the situation you were working in. What type of organization was it? What role did you hold at that organization? What were your duties, level, responsibilities and deliverables for that job?

> **Example:** *I was serving as the operations manager for a small paper converting and packaging organization. I was responsible for the safety, quality and productivity for a two machine plant that ran 24 hours/day with a total of 24 people in the operation. We were tasked with installing and starting up both of the pieces of equipment (worth $3 million) which required outside mechanical contractors, mechanical and electrical installation personnel and initial training of the operating staff in a 60-day time period.*

Your goal here is to paint a picture for the person reading your ACV so they can understand your point of reference and imagine themselves in a similar role. Notice that the cost of the equipment and the number of employees involved gives the reader perspective on how large the task was.

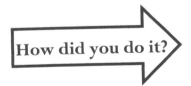

Focus on the tasks and skills that were required to complete the project. How did you decide what needed to be done and in what order? What resources were available to you and how did you decide when to use them? Did you ask for or need assistance from others?

Walk through step by step how you worked through this project with a keen eye on skills that you used in getting it done.

> **Example:** *First I evaluated the situation and created a timeline for the project to be completed by focusing on the date that we needed to be operational and "back planning" all the events from that date. I used Microsoft Project to create a timeline with tasks required and the order in which they needed to be done.*

I then identified tasks that required outside resources to complete and researched options for that support and created a tasks checklist for each of the people involved in the project to create clarity in what they needed to do and when. I created daily 15-minute Scrum (team update) meetings and weekly one-hour update leadership meeting to ensure clear communication and no surprises. I monitored outside vendors using weekly check in meetings to ensure we stayed on time and on budget.

How may skills could you pick out of that story? I'll cover skills soon. Mostly, this part of the ACV is to demonstrate how your skill sets, thinking, planning and actions brought success to this project.

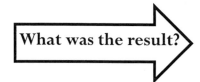 **What was the result?** Describe the result of your actions in a way that it is clear you created value for your organization.

Example: *This project was completed on time, within budget and met or exceeded quality parameters. The company met its startup dates and customers' needs and expectations.*

The best results will be measurable and easy to substantiate. Focus on time or money saved increased sales or decreased costs. Here are examples:

- ✓ Sales increases or the ability to create larger sales
- ✓ Increasing levels of responsibility
- ✓ Increased efficiency or reduced waste
- ✓ Creating new business relationships or partnerships
- ✓ Opening up new markets
- ✓ Removing internal or external conflicts or obstacles

> *It is important that your results can draw a direct line between your efforts and the positive outcome.*

Create shortened ACV statements	The last step is to turn that entire one page story into a much shorter version you can use going forward in many ways. You can use this abbreviated version of your ACV story on resumes and as answers to interview questions. These shorter versions will become the foundation for all of the work you do the rest of the way in this process so do your very best. This is your story so make it compelling!

Example: *I was responsible for all aspects regarding the installation and start-up of a $3 million paper converting line (what you did). Evaluated the situation and utilized the machine manufacturer, the construction company and the operating staff's expertise. Created a timeline for installation, identified tasks to be completed, and then assigned them to responsible parties with completion dates and held update meetings. (how you did it). The paper converting machine started up on time, within cost, and met a predetermined start-up production curve (the result).*

Spend A LOT of time on these as they will serve you well when it comes to preparing for an interview.

Keep these ideas in mind as you write:

Describe the situation you were in (What was your position or role? What type of organization or industry were you in? Were you managing people, a process or doing the actual work?)

Describe the problem or opportunity you addressed (What was the issue? How did you become aware of it? Were you responsible directly for carrying it through or serving as an active member of a team? What was the negative or anticipated consequence of not acting?)

Describe your actions to solve the problem or act on the opportunity (What options did you have? How did you decide on a course of action? What actions did you decide on and why? Did you act alone or did you act as part of a team? How did you implement your actions, and how was success measured?)

Describe the positive results of your actions (Were there increased sales or decreased costs? Were efficiencies improved? Was an employee developed? Were processes put in place? Did you find a new market?)

Write these statements and rehearse them as if you were talking to a complete stranger, because when you use this information in a networking or interview setting, you will be talking to someone who just met you!

You can have all the networking opportunities in the world, but unless you can share with people how to solve their problems, make their life easier, or help get them closer to the next bonus or goal, then networking is nothing more than shaking hands with strangers.

Stop here and write out your 7-10 work, school or life achievements in the format presented above. Do not continue without completing this assignment. On average this assignment will take the job seeker 3-4 hours to complete.

When you are finished, turn each one of them into a shortened ACV statement like the example above. These three sentence ACVs will be used in resumes, cover letters, networking briefs and interview preparation later in the process.

HSE Achievement Worksheet

1. Compete as a varsity NCAA collegiate athlete.

2. Helped my team achieve a 9th place national ranking in 2016.

3. Maintain a 3.5 GPA.

4. Serve as a project manager & board member for Badger Consulting.

5. Successfully completed an internship abroad at Bank of Ireland.

6. Speak French proficiently.

7. Spend time volunteering to give back to the community.

HSE Achievement Worksheet

HSE Achievement Worksheet

Shortened ACV Statements

Identify skills from your achievements

Next, create a list from your achievement (ACV) experiences that identify skills you have used in the workplace. Consider what skills were used to contribute toward each of your previously noted achievements. Below is a sample list of professional skills created by a former marketing manager at a large insurance firm:

✓ **Communication** (oral, formal public speaking, written, etc.)
✓ **Editing** (copy, writing, scripting, etc.)
✓ **Management** (project, people, etc.)
✓ **Marketing** (research, target or online marketing, focus groups, advertising)
✓ **Planning**
✓ **Supervising**

Here are some other skills commonly used in association with various business-related achievements:

✓ **Analysis**
✓ **Budgeting**
✓ **Coordination**
✓ **Cost-savings**
✓ **Design** (industrial, mechanical, interior, commercial, product, graphic/computer, etc.)
✓ **Development** (product, service, construction, fundraising, event, etc.)
✓ **Diagnostic**
✓ **Established** (system, process, procedure, event, form of recognition, policy, etc.)

✓ **Figure/Calculate** (a problem, a solution, etc.)
✓ **Instructed/Trained**
✓ **Leadership** (any reference to leading people or a process, project, etc.)
✓ **Negotiated**
✓ **Programmed** (processes, software, systems, networks, etc.)
✓ **Researched** (problems, case studies, improved processes, products, services, etc.)
✓ **Sold**
✓ **Troubleshoot**

Refer back to the ACV narratives that you wrote. Use the skills matrix on the next page to identify the skills associated with each of your achievements. A pattern will develop. You will see certain skills that are frequently associated with your achievements regardless of what they are or where they happened. This is important as your past successes leave clues to where your future successes will happen.

Do not proceed before this skills matrix is completed.

Skills Matrix

Refer back to your achievement or Ability to Create Value (ACV) Generator. Write those achievements across the top and use the Skills Matrix to identify the unique skills associated with each achievement. What patterns emerge? What skills do you use often? Your past successes leave clues to where your future successes will happen.

	Athlete	Team Ranking ↑	3.5 GPA	Badger Consulting	BoI Internship	Speak French	Volunteering					
Analyze	✓	✓	✓	✓	✓							5
Benchmark		✓										1
Budget			✓									1
Change/Improve	✓	✓	✓			✓	✓					5
Coordinate				✓								1
Communicate	✓	✓	✓	✓	✓		✓					6
Cost-Savings/Lean												0
Design					✓							1
Develop				✓	✓	✓						3
Diagnose												0
Edit				✓	✓							2
Establish/Accelerate												0
Forecast/Predict			✓									1
Figure/Calculate			✓									1
Instruct/Train				✓								1
Leadership	✓	✓		✓		✓						4
Logistics			✓	✓								2
Management			✓	✓								2
Marketing												0
Negotiate												0
Organize			✓	✓	✓							3
Program												0
Research					✓							1
Supervision				✓								1
Sales												0
Troubleshoot	✓	✓	✓	✓								4

Skills Matrix

Download a PDF version of this worksheet at www.myhumansearchengine.com

Find you Dynamic Skill Set (DSS)

Take a look at the skills matrix you completed. Add up the number of checks across from each of the skills on the matrix and put that number in the "total" column. You should see that some skills have been used frequently by you, while others were used seldom or not at all. Now identify the 10 skills that got the most checks in the "total" column. These are your demonstrated skill set.

This list includes the skills most frequently associated with your past achievements…but that doesn't necessarily mean that these are the skills you want as the core of your next position. Figuring that out requires a little cross referencing exercise. The purpose of the exercise is to identify the skills you want use regularly in your next position.

Take a look at the worksheet on the next page. You will see that the columns are labeled as:

The skills you're good at	*The skills you love to do*	*The skills you have been paid to do*

Finding that intersection of skills is the goal of this exercise

To put this in perspective, you may be good at some skills, but you may not enjoy using them. For example, consider negotiation skills. You may excel at the art of negotiation, yet your stress levels fly through the ceiling when you have to use this skill, causing sleepless nights. Conversely, you may love working on computer-based designs, yet those are not the competencies you are being paid for.

Now look at the 10 demonstrated skills from the last exercise. Look at the first one and evaluate it like this:

✓ **Did I love to do it?**

✓ **Was I good at it?**

✓ **Can I demonstrate this skill in examples to show how this creates value for an organization?**

Go through these questions with each of the 10 skills and list the skills that fall into at least two out of the three columns. While it would be great to only choose those that fit into all three columns, that will highly limit your outcome. Your goal at this point is to research possibilities, not to come to a final conclusion.

Dynamic Skill Set (DSS) Worksheet

List the **top 10 skills** identified from the Skills Matrix. Place an "x" under the columns that apply.

Skill Demonstrated	Good At	Like To Do	Paid To Do
Communicate	X		
Change/Improve	X	X	X
Analyze	X	X	X
Leadership	X		
Troubleshoot	X		X
Develop	X		X
Organize	X	X	X
Edit	X		X
Logistics			X
management			X
Design			X
Research	X	X	X

Make a final list of **4-8 skills** that are found in at least two of the three columns above. These are the ideal skills that will define your next job, or your **Dynamic Skill Set (DSS)**.

Change/Improve	
Analyze	
Organize	
Research	

Download a PDF version of this worksheet at www.myhumansearchengine.com

Now make a final list of which of the skills that ended up in at least two columns. It is important you have 4 to 8 skills on this list. As you move forward in the HSE Process you will refer to this list as your dynamic skill set (DSS).

Something should occur to you at this point. As you look at this list of skills you should be saying to yourself: "I would LOVE a job where I used these skills the majority of my day."

Where does that job exist? That is the basis for the next phase of the process.

DO NOT continue until you have completed your DSS!

CHAPTER 5: SKILLS MATTER

Jobs that use Your Dynamic Skill Set (DSS)

Through the Venn diagram activity, you now have a sharper understanding of the ideal skills that will define your next job. Now, you can focus on roles that need these skills. This is the point where I see one of the biggest revelations from jobseekers that use the HSE Process. A jobseeker's view of the world goes from… there's nothing out there… to WOW, where do I start? Remember, jobseekers are generally unaware of 60-85% of the jobs that are available. Your research will be used to identify jobs where your DSS is valued and rewarded.

> ### *Sample of Intersected Skills*

With a clear set of skills in mind, now create a list of "jobs" that require your talents. Let's look at an example below of the Venn diagram from a jobseeker that completed this three-step process. At the intersection of the three circles, assume that the Venn diagram pinpoints the following skills: **researching, writing, training** and **public speaking.**

In this example, the jobseeker was previously a quality manager at a manufacturing company. As a traditional jobseeker, he would likely pursue his next role by concentrating on words and concepts like quality and management (right from his previous title). Conversely, if this jobseeker used the HSE Process, he would look for roles that focused on **researching, writing, training,** and **public speaking.**

The HSE Process expands the breadth of job options as a result of this jobseeker's DSS. He could look at roles that include a college instructor, a grant writer, a non-profit programming specialist or executive director, a corporate trainer, a marketing research professional, or a research and development director, to name a few.

The next exercise will help you determine what types of positions value your skills. It will allow you to begin to see all of your work come together, how you can provide value in ways you may have never thought of before and begin to see yourself and your future in a new light.

The Five Job Postings Exercise

1. Identify your Dynamic Skill Set
2. Go to a large online job search site like Monster or Indeed and set the parameters for a nationwide job search
3. Search for jobs by "key words". Enter one of the skills from you DSS list. (for the above example, the jobseeker would enter **training** in the search field and after that the other DSS terms…in this case writing, training and public speaking).
4. Enter the rest of the terms from your DSS list.

In the example training may appear in job postings for trainer, consultant, coach, coordinator or specialized areas like safety, management, technical development, etc. You will find that many different jobs use the skills listed on your DSS and that will begin to open your eyes to career possibilities you may not have considered.

Don't limit yourself to local jobs as part of this activity. You are just doing research, so if you live in Texas, but find a job posting for a position in Ohio, no problem. You are not going to apply to the job in Ohio, but you will be creating a profile for jobs like this that exist within 10 or 20 miles of where you live. *Becoming aware of roles that value your DSS you hadn't considered is the goal of this exercise.*

You must broaden your scope of possibilities. Consider industries you have never thought of before. After all, at this point your job search is just a research project – and from now on that's how I will refer to it. You will begin to see that your skills are valued by many different companies, by many different industries and in many different roles.

That's the freedom of the HSE Process... it's all about possibilities. There will be plenty of time to investigate each of the jobs that interest you during the research phase, which begins in the next chapter. Perhaps for the first time in a long time you will be asking yourself, "What do I want?" instead of, "What do I have to take?"

The last step of the 5 jobs exercise is a critical one –

> Print out each of the 5 jobs that you identified for this exercise. Now highlight the words and phrases that drew you to that job. These words and phrases demonstrate traits of the position that you eventually want to land...we need to start creating the profile of the position we are looking for by paying attention to the words and phrases in these target job postings.

1. Senior Planning & Business Analyst – Strategy
2. Financial Analyst / Data Analyst
3. Business Analyst / Consultant
4. Analytic Consultant
5. Finance Research Analyst

Job Objective Statements

The last part of the Definition Phase of the HSE Process asks you to come up with several clear objectives to start your search. This is referred to as an Objective Statement. The format of an Objective Statement looks like this:

"A _____position involving _____, _____, and _____ for a(n) _____ company focused on _____."

Example 1: "A <u>lean facilitator</u> position involving <u>identifying</u> and <u>eliminating waste</u>, <u>implementing Six Sigma strategies</u> and <u>conducting kaizen events</u> for a <u>progressive manufacturing</u> company focused on <u>world- class products."</u>

Notice two aspects about the above example:

1. Industry-specific words are used in the Objective Statement so people from the field will quickly identify your expertise. These words indicate to people a level of knowledge about the industry and a competency that you have served in that field.

2. The Objective Statement allows the person with whom you will be networking to immediately identify people that have similar backgrounds or experiences. This person can then draw connections in his or her mind to others who "live in that world."

Example 2: "A <u>sales manager</u> position involving <u>identifying market segment opportunities, teaching needs-based selling techniques</u> and <u>increasing lead penetration through aggressive new customer prospecting</u> for an <u>international consumer goods</u> company focused on <u>outstanding service</u>."

Now, your turn! Write two possible Objective Statements based on the skills and experience you have identified so far. After developing your objectives, test them on a few people who you already know and see if they can name a person or company representing that kind of work. Don't worry about asking them to connect you to anyone yet. Just see if your Objective Statements lead those who are WILLING to help you with your search identify others in their "mental Rolodex" who might be ABLE to help you.

Do not continue until you have completed your objective statements using the next worksheet

Please note here that your objective statement is much more than something to put at the top of your resume. It is designed and written in a way that it will be used to guide your entire research project. It will be what helps you decide what companies and industries to consider. It will help shape the profile of the organization you ultimately go to work for. It will allow you to decide "YES or NO" when considering whether to apply for a job. This is your "North Star" as far as your research project goes

Creating Your Objective Statement

Your Objective Statement will define and guide your entire HSE job search. It will help shape what <u>you</u> are looking for in your next opportunity, and allow <u>you</u> to decide "YES" or "NO" when considering to apply for a job. Write your Objective Statement carefully and make sure it is a good representation of what <u>you</u> want in your next position.

"A _____ position involving _____, _____, and _____ for a(n) _____ company focused on _____."

First, let's brainstorm the <u>type of position</u> you're looking for in 1-2 keyword phrases:

Analyst	Planning
Consultant	Strategy

Now, what are the <u>industry-specific skills</u> you will bring to the position? These words indicate to people a level of knowledge about the industry and a competency that you have served in that field.

Data Analytics	Financial Research
Database Research	Economic Analysis
Strategic Thinking	Compiling of Information
Problem-Solving	Communication

Finally, what kind of company and/or company culture do you want to work for? Remember, this isn't necessarily the organization or industry you came from, but the world you <u>want</u> to work in next.

Organized	Industry-Leading
Structured	Business-Oriented

Download a PDF version of this worksheet at www.myhumansearchengine.com

Definition Overview

1. Use an online tool to understand your Myers-Briggs Type Indicator profile.

2. Write out in detail 7-10 work-related achievements. Based on your experience these could also be education-related or volunteer experiences. These achievements should be written out in the format of: What did you do, how did you do it, and what was the result. These statements should contain significant detail to fill a page or more in length. Focus mostly on the "How did you do it" section.

3. Use the checklist to identify which specific skills were used in making each of these achievements happen. Make a specific and inclusive list of all skills used in each achievement as these will be important in the next steps.

4. Make a list of the skills that show up often in each of your achievements (DSS).

5. Make a list of each of the skills that show up in at least half of the achievements.

6. Identify the skills that fall into at least two of the three categories of Good at, Like to Do, Paid to do.

7. Go to a large online job search engine and identify 5 jobs that interest you while completely ignoring how much they pay, where they are geographically, or whether you are actually qualified to do them. Print these out and now identify the words or phrases that draw you to this job. Take note of the duties and responsibilities in these positions. They reflect the duties and responsibilities that need to be part of your next position.

8. Create 2 Objective Statements using industry specific terminology as laid out in chapter 12.

9. List the "industry specific" terminology and skills that you will be using in your message going forward.

CHAPTER 6: RESEARCH BEGINS

Test your job search hypothesis

As with any good research project, the objective statement you have created is really just a hypothesis…an educated guess. The research portion of HSE Process is all about testing that hypothesis and adjusting it based on what you learn through your research.

Now that you have an idea of the skills you want to be using every day in your next role, it is important to identify who values those skills. The core of any sales training will tell you that a sale is made when the benefits of a product or service are shown to solve the problem of the customer. Match one with the other and you won't have to sell anything to anyone; the customer will CHOOSE to buy! Finding a new job using the HSE Process is no different.

There are two steps in this part of the process:

✓ Identify job types and industries that value your skill set.
✓ Identify problems in those jobs that you are uniquely able to solve.

Your goal is to create a profile of the type of organization that has the kinds of problems that you can solve so that you can identify them in your geographical area

This is the moment when I begin to challenge what you THINK you know about the job opportunities around you. Take a look at the skill set you developed through the Venn diagram. These are the skills you will be using 90% of the time in your next position. Now it's time to find them in organizations around you…even ones you have never considered or heard of.

Step 1: Identify job types and industries that value your skills

Go back to the popular internet job search sites you used earlier. In the keyword search area of whatever job search site you selected, enter one of the skills you came up with in your DSS… like negotiation. Make sure that the site is searching in *your local area code*, or close to it. Type "negotiation" into the keyword search pane and hit enter.

What types of positions do you see? What types of industries do those open positions represent? Did the search also bring up names of organizations you have never heard of? What other responsibilities does that position require, and do you have those skills?

Now enter another skill into the search pane on the job search site. Ask yourself the same questions as in the previous example using the skill of negotiation. What other industries and organizations are you becoming aware of as a result of this exercise?

Two important conclusions can be drawn from the first step in this chapter:

First, you will find that some organizations are currently looking for people with your skills. **Second**, you will become aware of many companies and organizations you have never heard of. Remember, one of the biggest problems jobseekers have is they are unaware of at least 85% of all of the companies within 30 miles of them. You can't work for an organization you don't know exists.

This step in the process will make you aware of hundreds of organizations around you. In my seminars, I often ask people how many organizations exist within 30 miles of my hometown Appleton, Wisconsin. The guesses range from 500 to 5,000. The actual number is more than 30,000! That fact is met with startled looks of disbelief…even by people that have lived their whole lives there.

Then I ask people to start naming all of those organizations. In a room full of 100 people who have lived in Appleton their whole lives, including me, we struggle to name more than 50… that's right, the group misses 29,950 possible organizations. The point is made. What possibilities are out there that you (and most other jobseekers) don't know exist?

During the process of identifying these roles, you will also begin to notice that your skill set is valued in more than one industry. Jobseekers have an almost knee jerk reaction that leads them to return to the industry that they came from, but skill sets cross industry lines. As a former operations manager in the paper industry, I now know that the skills I used to manage production would have been valued in the production of eye glasses, cell phones, or car tires. The ability to manage teams of people, increase productivity, reduce waste, and improve safety continues to be valued by every manufacturing company around.

The same could be said for the ability to sell, design or teach.

You will quickly find that the only one keeping you in the same industry is you.

Step 2: Identify problems you are uniquely able to solve

Never forget that hiring managers hire people to solve their problems, make their life easier and get them closer to their goals.

In order to present yourself in a way that is attractive to an employer, you must define how you can create value for them.

Look to your Achievement Statements for problems you have solved in the past. Do other industries value solving those problems? Which companies struggle with the same types of issues? Does your work save time, create sales opportunities, build teams, organize initiatives or manage projects, to name a few?

Consider the last organization you worked for. Now look at its *customers, competitors and vendors.* These organizations will likely value your skills as well. If these organizations do the same type of work as your last employer, wouldn't it make sense they would value you as well? Wouldn't your ability to solve problems for one of their competitors be of interest to them? If you created value for your last employer's customers, wouldn't those customers be interested in a conversation with you? Your ability to demonstrate solving problems specific to that industry would be interesting to everyone in that industry, wouldn't it?

A broad objective is like having no objective at all...

Unfortunately, you have been taught to use this type of phrase to anyone that would listen:

"I am willing and able to solve any problem in any organization regardless of its industry, size or structure."

While that sounds like it is casting a broad net that encompasses all employers, it is really an unrealistic statement that business people see through in a second.

Using this type of opening is one of the **single biggest mistakes** jobseekers make. An unfocused statement like the one above makes it impossible for you to focus your search on any specific organization. It also makes it impossible for people who are WILLING to help you with your job search to be ABLE to help you. Lastly, and most destructively for your search, this opening makes it sound as if you are desperate and are ready to accept any job that is willing to pay you to come to work. It is hard to be seen as valuable when the message you are sending is that of a beggar. Make sure your job search objective is clear enough that it can be understood by anyone.

Finding your test audience

In your research project you will be utilizing one of the most overlooked resources…people you already know who are WILLING to help you on your search. Your next task is to create lists of people you know who fit into one of three categories. Don't worry, you won't be hitting them up for a job. I often say "people want to help you with your job search but they don't know how, so you need to teach them how." You don't need them to "get you in" somewhere or get your resume to HR. What you need from them is their **advice, guidance and feedback.** Later I'll explain what this means and how it will be incredibly helpful to you.

> **Three critical lists for your HSE job search:**
> **"Who thinks you're awesome?" list**
> **ABC list**
> **1000/1000 list**

List 1: Who thinks you're awesome?

The word networking strikes fear into even the most seasoned business person. Preconceived (but incorrect) ideas about networking keep most people from ever really attempting it. One of the false notions is that networking has to do with meeting strangers and trying to get something from them (information, a job lead, a sale, etc.). No wonder people don't want to do it! What if instead of that, you focus your initial conversations with people who already have judged you as good enough personally and professionally?

Think about it…who could be more WILLING to help you get back into the workforce than someone who has already worked side by side with you? They know your skills and your personality, your drive and your integrity. So let's make a list of people who fit into that category- The *"who thinks you're awesome?"* list.

Think about your previous 3 or 4 school or work situations and make a list of former:

Peers and coworkers

Supervisors

Mentors

HR managers (they hired you once, didn't they?)

Customers

Vendors

Salespeople

Teachers

People you attended school with (Classmates)

Volunteers

This should be a free flowing list of EVERYBODY who fits into those categories…don't spend any time guessing how they will help you during your search. Come back to the list several times after you write it. Review old job records (like performance reviews) to reignite your memory. Going forward you will find that this list might be the only list you truly need. It will make networking for your next role go from approaching strangers with fear to a virtual family reunion!

List 2: ABC list

Next you will make a list of people you know who:

✓ Have **hiring authority** in any industry or **own a business** (A List)

✓ **Currently work in the industry you want to work in, but have no hiring authority** (B List)

✓ **Represent anyone who is willing to discuss your job search with you** (C List).

Before you start your lists, gather contacts from your email, your church, past employers and co-workers, neighbors, etc. Don't judge or evaluate the names you write—just brainstorm. You will evaluate and organize these contacts later in the process.

Now, start creating your A List **of people who have hiring authority or own a business:**

It's important to have A List individuals because they will understand exactly what you are doing. People who fit into the A list category would never look in the want ads or on the internet for their next job. They would go about it in the same way that you are being taught in this workbook. You are likely not going to ask any of these A List people to help you get a job, so relax.

Do people who own a business understand networking? You bet! These business owners don't have thousands of dollars a month to spend on advertising. If they don't network for clients, their business dies.

Once your A List is complete, develop your B List of people who currently **work in the industry you want to work in, but have no hiring authority:**

The fact that these people have no hiring authority is an important point here. You don't have to worry about putting pressure on them to get you a job, because they don't have the authority to give you one! What they have is industry information and connections, which is what you really need from them. Focus on former co-workers, vendors, customers, professional colleagues, teachers and peers.

Once your A and B Lists are complete, create the C List based on **anyone who is willing to discuss your job search with you:**

The only real standard here is that the people on your C List are WILLING to help you with your search, like friends, neighbors, former co-workers, other workplace colleagues, etc. Don't worry at all about how these people will help you. That they are WILLING to help you is the only thing that matters. They want to help you with your search, but don't know how. You are going to teach them how.

Your C list will consist of friends and family, people you volunteer or serve on boards with. People from your church or community go here. Former high school or college friends you haven't thought of in years will be brought back to mind and should be added to this list.

List 3: The 1000/1000 list

After you have created your ABC List, there is a final list of people who you need to capture. Don't worry; this will be a very short list... probably three or four people at the most.

The definition of your 1000/1000 List:

If you were 1000 miles away from home, in jail, on Christmas Eve and needed $1000 bail—who could you call and without a moment's hesitation, this person would grab his or her checkbook, leave his/her family and jump in the car and start driving on Christmas Eve to come bail you out?

This is a pretty short list, isn't it? If you are like most people, you will be able to count the number of these individuals on one hand.

You have just created a list of the first people with whom you will meet, and it's not all intimidating. This means you won't be meeting with strangers. As we say in HSE Process: start easy, start close to home, but start today.

These lists integrate two important elements for jobseekers that I will explain in more detail as you move through the process:

You will learn how these two elements interact later. In general terms, your goal is to ask people who are WILLING to help you to introduce you to people who are ABLE to help you. This is one of the real breakthroughs of the HSE Process.

> *People who are WILLING to help you and People who are ABLE to help you.*

Use the following sheets to make each of these lists

Who Thinks You're Awesome List

Who could be more WILLING to help you get back into the workforce than someone who has already worked side by side with you? They know your skills and your personality, your drive and your integrity. In sum, they think you're awesome!

Think about your past 3-4 jobs, volunteer roles, or educational experiences. Who did you click with? Who did you have a great working relationship with? Who did you solve problems for? Who did you help out in a pinch? This should be a free flowing list of people inside and outside of the organization (colleagues, supervisors, HR managers, vendors, salespeople, etc.).

Remember: Don't pre-judge, just write!

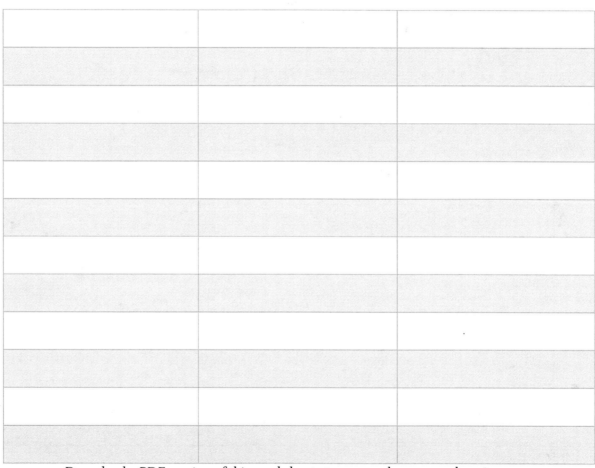

Download a PDF version of this worksheet at www.myhumansearchengine.com

1000 / 1000 List

If you were 1,000 miles away from home, in jail, on Christmas Eve and needed $1,000 bail—who would come to help without a moment's hesitation? **This list will be short**, but represents the people who are most WILLING to help you in your job search.

ABC List

Before you start, gather contacts from your email, LinkedIn, church, past employers, former co-workers, neighbors, etc. **This is a brainstorming exercise—no one is off limits**. We'll evaluate and organize these contacts later on. Don't pre-judge, just write!

A List: People with hiring authority in any industry <u>OR</u> own a business	B List: People who currently work in the industry you want to work in, but have no hiring authority	C List: Anyone willing to discuss your job search with you

Download a PDF version of this worksheet at www.myhumansearchengine.com

CHAPTER 7: DESIGNING THE NEXT JOB

Looking Forward by Examining the Past

Before you can identify where you want to go, it is important for you to analyze where you have come from. It is said, "Those who do not learn from the past are destined to relive it." This is very true of jobseekers. It is time to analyze your last position to help define what you want for your next position.

If you were completely happy in your last position (but were perhaps displaced), then your search should be relatively easy. Just identify the customers, competitors and vendors associated with that company. These customers, competitors and vendors will likely have the same types of problems and opportunities your last employer had. That is a relatively easy list to make. Make sure, however, that you truly enjoyed that position before completing this list.

But what if you were unhappy in your last position and want to make sure you don't end up in a similar place? If that's the case, it's time for you to define the job *and* situation you are looking for in your next career.

If you were unhappy in your last job, one of three assertions has to be TRUE:

> 1. You were in the right job, but the wrong situation
>
> 2. You were in the wrong job, but the right situation
>
> 3. You were in the wrong job and the wrong situation

Here are examples of the terms noted above in the three instances of being unhappy in a previous job:

 Your "job" as stated above refers to the duties, tasks and responsibilities of your last position. What were you functionally doing each day? What was expected of you, and what actions did you need to take to fulfill those expectations? You could also refer to the terms that were discussed earlier that we refer to as "what skills did you use each day to accomplish your tasks?"

 Your "situation" refers to the setting in which you were doing your job. It refers to the mission, values and actions of your last employer. In other words, what was the internal dynamic like in regard to people and practices? What beliefs did your last employer hold? Were their employee assets valued, or was the staff not valued much at all? What was their leadership style?

Here is a sample of the first assertion: If you were a salesperson who loves sales (right job), but were working for a company with deceptive sales practices (wrong situation), it would lead to stress and unhappiness in your job.

Here is a sample portrayal from the second assertion: If you were working for a great organization that highly valued its employees (right situation), but you were doing mechanical repairs each day even though you had no desire to do those repairs (wrong job), then you would again find yourself in a very stressful place for different reasons.

Before researching possible employers you might want to work for, it is critical to be able to define a career that is BOTH the right job and the right situation for you. Running from the manufacturing industry which you loved-(right job) because you had a horrible boss (wrong situation) will drive you from a profession that you like and are good at just because of a bad supervisor. If this was the case, your research project would be all about finding a manufacturer to work for that was known for valuing its employees.

Start asking yourself these questions as part of the research component. These will be the questions that you will seek to answer during the HSE Process:

- ✓ **Who in my opinion has the best job I have ever seen and that I have interest in?**

- ✓ **What are the really great companies to work for in the area based on feedback from employees who work there and/or from companies that do business with them?**

- ✓ **How do people get to work for one of those really good organizations?**

Lastly, I want to make this point. Often when I am working with new students or clients to identify why they left their last job or where they are headed (career-wise), I need to ask them a simple question: "With this new job, are you moving *toward* something good, or are you running *away* from something bad?" Honestly answering this question will keep you from accepting the first opportunity that comes your way if it doesn't fit what you are looking for.

Now, write a description of the "right job in the right situation" for a role you are seeking. Don't relive the past...reinvent your future! Keep this description with all of your other HSE homework as you continue your research.

> **STOP NOW AND WRITE YOUR DESCRIPTION OF THE RIGHT JOB IN THE RIGHT SITUATION FOR YOUR NEXT POSITION ON THE FOLLOWING WORKSHEET. Base this description on duties, level, responsibilities, industries, daily activities and deliverables (the measurable end result of your work).**

Designing the Right Job, Right Situation

If you could design the right job in the right situation, what would it look like? What would you be doing? Who would you be working with? This is your ultimate dream. Don't relive the past—reinvent it!

1. Description of duties

2. Level of responsibility-will you be managing people or process?

3. Industry or organization

4. Daily activities

5. Deliverables (what is the positive, measurable result of your work?)

Download a PDF version of this worksheet at www.myhumansearchengine.com

What problems can you solve?

...And who has those problems? I'd like you to clear your mind just for a minute before you read this next sentence. It is that important to your search...ready?

> "People hire people to solve their problems, make their lives easier and to get them closer to their next goal or bonus."

I've said it before, but my belief is that if you get nothing else from this process, this one idea will be enough to change the course of your search. The only thing that matters here is to identify people who have the problems you are ABLE to solve and to meet with them so that they can see that you are worth considering for their organization.

Think of your own life. When you hire a babysitter or someone to care for your lawn, why do you hire them? Because the value they bring to you is greater than the value of the money that you have to pay them. Whether the decision is about a $9/hour babysitter or a $90,000/year marketing position...the same rules apply. So again...

What problems are you able to solve? Who has those problems? Finding a legitimate way to get in front of those people is all there is to an effective proactive job search. So how do you go about identifying the people and organizations that need you?

Research tools & databases – Creating target lists

In solving the second problem of job search (you are unaware of at least 85% of available job opportunities), there are tools at your local library that will enable you to expand your scope of possible opportunities. The key to unlocking these tools is a little thing called SIC (Standard Industrial Classification) codes.

Simply start by asking a librarian to show you the research materials that are available for jobseekers. Libraries are not archaic. Today's libraries offer a wealth of resources thanks to technology and inter-connective functionality with other learning resource centers designed to bridge information. Librarians conduct research for a living so ask them for help!

Have your librarian guide you to databases such as *Hoover's* or *Reference USA* (online data bases) or your state's manufacturing and service guides (published resource books on the library shelves). Whether you are searching for companies using an online database or looking in a hardcover book, the goal is the same. You are now identifying companies that you never knew existed in your industry or area of expertise. That's where SIC codes come in.

These codes are assigned by the government to each industry for purposes of categorizing organizations into groups. Every body shop has the same SIC code. Every college has the same SIC code. Every computer repair shop has the same SIC code, and so on.

So, now you realize there are thousands, perhaps tens of thousands, of businesses within 30 miles of your home. This is both a blessing and a curse. The blessing is that there are a lot of organizations you haven't considered working for because you didn't know they existed. The curse is how do you start sorting through them all? Using SIC codes solves this problem.

Do you now see why this is so important to your search? Before you can start identifying all of the organizations that value your skill set, you need to know their SIC codes. Once you know the SIC code, you can go online to find a list of all of the companies that are categorized under that classification.

In the Appleton, Wisconsin region, manufacturing is big business. This region makes up the third-largest manufacturing sector in the United States. There are about a half of dozen well-known paper manufacturing companies that exist within 30 miles of my home, but there are dozens of smaller companies that represent the same industry. Most people have never heard of these smaller businesses or even considered them as potential employers.

The SIC code for paper manufacturing and converting is 2621. More than 70 organizations are listed under that SIC code within 30 miles of my home. If my expertise were paper manufacturing, I'd better know all of the companies that could use my services before I start my search. Every jobseeker is going to run to the paper companies that everyone already knows exists. Only HSE jobseekers will be approaching great paper companies that are lesser known… and those businesses may have great jobs that are also not known of.

Create the profile of your ideal company

The next step in the HSE Process is creating a profile for the company you want to work for. If you create a profile of organizations you desire to connect with, you make it very easy for others to identify people or companies that fit that profile. Again, getting people who you are networking with to be able to narrow down the 500 people and 100 organizations that they have in their "mental Rolodex" is key. This is how, in part, you will receive direct referrals from them. In order to empower people who are WILLING to help you become ABLE to help you, creating this profile is a critical step.

In your profile you must define:

✓ **The size of the organization in terms of gross sales or number of employees.**

✓ **Is the organization privately held or publicly held?**

✓ **Is the organization a service or manufacturing organization (or other)?**

✓ **What industries do they mainly serve?**

✓ **Is it a for-profit or non-profit organization?**

Once you create a profile of companies you want to learn more about, you have taken a huge step in identifying which organizations are real possibilities for employment. Now, before you move on, create a profile of the organization you want to work for next (yes, your dream job). Definition is the key. Remember the old saying, "If you don't know where you are going, any road will get you there."

'The organization' that you want to work for has now been defined. This information can now be broadened to create a Target List.

A Target List includes all of the organizations within your geographical region (or beyond, if desired) that you would either **like to work for** or **need the skills and abilities that you have.** It's irrelevant if these companies have current posted job openings or not. Create the Target List. Aim for at least 20.

Here are some helpful tips when developing your Target List:

List all organizations that you already know fit your professional objective.
Ask people who do the kind of work you want to do for names of their competitors (sounds funny, but think about it… they'll either not blink an eye and give you some names, or they'll think twice about maybe wanting to explore your credentials).
Share your Target List with individuals on your ABC List and seek their input.
Ask friends and family about organizations they have worked for or have done business with.
Research organizations using manufacturing and service directories (referenced above).
Request employer reports and employment resources from your local college or technical college (many people don't realize that a large repository of companies that regularly hire exist at this level of higher education due to two-year colleges' core mission of training for employment and their direct relationship to employers).

Now, research each company on your Target List to see how they are doing, what they are doing and how they do business. The goal is to discover enough information about each one that you could have a quality conversation about the organization. This research will also help you determine which of these organizations have values and goals that match your principles. When you have done this research, prioritize your Target List into the order of organizations you would most like to work for.

Visit each organization's website, ask your ABC List individuals about them, Google them to check recent news and use your connections to schedule a cup of coffee with someone who knows about these organizations to find even more information. Chances are these people may even know someone at one of the organizations on your Target List they can refer you to in order to further your research.

The goal of making this Target List is not only to give you an idea of the organizations you would be interested in contacting, **but it will also be used in all of your conversations during the rest of the HSE Process**. Showing this list to people during conversations will help them clearly understand the kind of organization you are seeking. You couldn't ask for a better conversation starter!

Research Overview

1. Begin by identifying the types of positions you have in your Objective Statement. What industries use those types of positions (find their common SIC code)? What job titles fit the type of work that you have defined? What are the common responsibilities of a person with that type of job (look at job postings across the country for that type of job and find common words or requirements that keep showing up in the postings)? What different names are used for this type of job in various industries?

2. Use your local library to research which organizations exist within a 30-mile radius of your desired location that have the SIC codes you have identified. You will be shocked at the number of organizations you were not aware of. Research sites like *Hoovers* or *Reference USA* (they are paid sites that the library, local college or university might have access to for free). Books like your state's manufacturing and service guides will be available and use the same SIC code system.

3. Create a profile of the type of organization you want to work for. Consider variables like number of employees, for-profit/non-profit, privately/publicly held, established or newer company, industry, service or manufacturing based, etc. Creating and sticking to this profile will not only make you aware of organizations that you didn't know existed, but it will also ensure you are only focusing on organizations that would be a good fit for you. Remember, if you don't know where you are going, any road will get you there.

4. Cross reference your organizational profile with the organizations you become aware of by doing the research. Then create a Target List of organizations. These are not necessarily ones you want to work for; they are resources that you would like to learn more about using the HSE Process.

5. After creating your Target List of companies, continue your research on each of these organizations to become aware of their employees, recent news and events that involve the company, products or services and competitors. Remember, this information will help you identify other organizations that would value your skills and experience.

6. Share your Target List with people on your 1000/1000 List and on your ABC List. Make them aware that you are researching these organizations and at some point would appreciate their help connecting with people who know more about them.

7. Evaluate the list of target companies. Read their websites and news stories. What common words or themes do they use in their value or mission statements? What common problems or opportunities do they share? Are those ideas reflected in your skill set?

8. Use your ABC List and 1000/1000 List. Make sure to create this list one day and then revisit it a couple days later to ensure that other people WILLING to help you make the list (you may not think of everyone in one list-making session). Keep your ABC List close to your phone or e-mail so you can add to it as you go through this process.

9. Cross reference your ABC List and 1000/1000 list against your Target List of organizations. Are there any commonalities?

10. The goal is research through discussions with people in the job type or industry you have targeted. What problems do they face and how would your skill set solve them?

CHAPTER 8: MARKETING

Become your own recruiter!

Each time I begin to speak at a seminar, teach a class or work with an individual client, the conversation eventually turns to networking… and the dialogue never fails to surprise me. The moment "networking" comes up I see a chorus line of eye rolls. The response to the subject is usually something like "everyone knows they are looking for a job". I congratulate them and then ask how that is working for them so far.

I tell them that their efforts aren't so much networking as they are acting like a beggar on the street holding a cup. This is the moment I can begin to reshape the strategies of jobseekers for the rest of their life.

I'd like to clear up a common misconception about what *Human Search Engine* networking is and what it is not. Remember, I have explained several times how the average person finds virtually everything of value through some sort of networking already…and using it to find a job is not much different. The only difference between "everyday" networking and *HSE* networking is the focus. Now the focus is on your career and your future, and is tailored and scripted to meet those very objectives. Lastly, HSE networking is planned, practiced and executed in a logical and sequential manner to create a stated end result: Getting you in front of people who need you. You will not be asking for a job, you will be asking for advice, guidance and feedback on the research you are doing.

Human Search Engine is NOT:	*Human Search Engine IS:*
Telling your friends that you are looking for a job and to let you know if they hear of anything.	A research project. After defining who you are, your first goal is to execute a job search "research project" before looking for a new position.
Randomly "getting in front of" important or influential people so they can hire you.	Planning and executing a string of logical conversations that progress in an orderly direction toward solving the <u>two biggest problems of job search:</u> 1) No one knows you exist, and 2) You are currently unaware of at least 85% of the organizations that could hire you now.
Enlisting every recruiter in a 30-mile radius.	
Having random conversations with anyone and then hoping that they "put in a good word" for you.	All about conversing with the <u>right</u> people who are WILLING to help you with your search, while teaching them how to get you to people who are then ABLE to help you with your search.
Dropping off your resume to anyone willing to accept it and then waiting for them to call.	

Networking the wrong way can hurt you

Now, let's explore some more general common misconceptions about the value of networking and describe why networking the wrong way (not the HSE way) can actually **hurt your job search efforts.**

It is important to understand that by the time jobseekers come to one of my seminars or workshops, almost of all of them have been doing their job search independently for an average of three months. These are intelligent and successful people in their own right, who are likely going to be great hires for some organization. So if these people are smart and accomplished, why do they struggle with their job search?

The answer is…the very traits that made them successful in their careers up to this point are now creating barriers for their job search. The ideas and methodology that got them hired and promoted in the past are now the very things that are keeping them unemployed. Let me explain.

There are no straight lines in networking

Most organizations greatly value the ability to get from point A to point B in the most direct way using the shortest (or least expensive) possible path. With this in mind, many jobseekers are focused on trying to get in front of people who are ABLE to hire them in directly. They assume they will be able to overwhelm these individuals with their skills and personality and this "important person" will be compelled to hire them. It sounds logical, but IT JUST DOESN'T WORK.

Why would that important person meet with you unless you have been referred to him or her by someone they already know and trust? The idea that a CEO or president of a company will receive a call or email from a COMPLETE STRANGER and drop everything to meet with them is a beautiful dream…but it just isn't true.

Again, look at your own life. How do you react to an unsolicited email or phone call? Like most people you never get to the message because unsolicited contacts don't normally have your best interest in mind. That email or phone message gets deleted and the letter goes into the trash.

But what if you received an email from a good friend of yours recommending this person or this service? Wouldn't that change everything?

Remember, networking is not about getting in front of the most people; it's about getting in front of the right people who need you to solve their problems.

Employing the help of others during your search

It's important to accept that no matter how much authority or power you wielded in previous jobs, you are now dependent on the help of others in your job search. You don't have control over anything other than your actions to market yourself to people and organizations that have the problems you can uniquely solve. This can be a very tough pill to swallow for people... especially if they really carried some clout in their last job or in previous careers. I even have a name for this type of jobseeker: a PIP, or "Previously Important Person."

PIPs often deny the idea that they need help from anybody. They will say, "Don't you know who I am?" I often respond accordingly by asking, "You mean, don't I know who you were?" This is a humbling moment for even the most successful PIP.

I don't say it to be mean, but it does serve as a gentle kick in the pants. It's a realization for a PIP that his/her search will be based on who they are...not on who they were. It is a moment when they realize their lack of success in job search is due to going it alone. They also slowly begin to understand the most important precursor of the HSE Process: *Be humble, be sincere and ask for help.*

Once they realize they need to ask for the help of people they already know personally and professionally, their "luck" quickly changes. In addition, they find that these old acquaintances are more than WILLING to help them once they know how.

One of my favorite sayings is: *People want to help you with your job search, but they don't know how. You need to teach them how.* Once your former peers and current friends understand they do not need to know of any open jobs or know any important people, they will fall all over themselves to help. So what do you need to teach them to help you with your HSE research project?

Whether it's during my job search sessions or working one-on-one with clients, the responses I hear about networking are predictable and generally revolve around:

It's what you THINK you know about NETWORKING for a job that keeps you unemployed!

- ✓ **I'm already doing that, but it hasn't worked so far.**
- ✓ **I want to make real progress with my job search, not spend my time having random conversations with strangers.**
- ✓ **I don't really know any important people who can get me a job.**
- ✓ **I have no desire to cold call on a dozen businesses and try to get them to interview me.**

These responses are all too revealing. You see, in job search it's "what you think you know" that gets you into the most trouble.

Most jobseekers have preconceived notions such as:

✓ **The media telling us how bad the job market is (Bad news sells a lot of newspapers!).**
✓ **Networking has to do with talking to strangers.**
✓ **Large companies are impossible to get in to.**
✓ **Smaller companies don't pay anything.**
✓ **What worked in our last job search will automatically work again.**

The hardest part of a job search might be admitting that what you "know" might not be true. If you're going about your next career using the HSE Process, the truth is:

✓ **It's not "the world's" fault that you can't find a job.**
✓ **Everyone needs help from others during a job search.**
✓ **Asking the right people to help you (and knowing how) is a learned skill.**
✓ **You are unaware of 85% of the organizations that could hire you.**
✓ **Your ego could be getting in the way (trying to do it alone).**
✓ **There is an entirely different way to search for a job, but it is NOT new; businesses have used this process for decades to launch new products and services.**

It makes sense that if a person has climbed the corporate ladder through sheer will and determination on his/her own part, the act of asking for help during a job search will be very hard. Harder yet is knowing you have been out of work for three, six, nine months or even a year, and that the world seems to be spinning along just fine without you.

Willing vs. Able: A Short Story

Imagine for a moment I asked you to go out and network to get a $10,000 loan for a really great business idea. If you are like most people, your mind will go to two places almost simultaneously.

1. **"I don't know anybody who has that type of money to loan out."**

2. **"Who is going to trust me enough to lend me that kind of money even if they have it?"**

Each question represents your actual thoughts of:

Who is WILLING to help you find the money?

Who is actually ABLE to lend you that type of money?

Most people would begin to focus on the second question, "Who is actually ABLE to lend you that type of money?" Business philosophy says that the most efficient way to get a loan is to talk to people you believe would have that type of money to lend. You might make lists of successful people, business owners, bankers, people you read about who got inheritances, etc. Talking to people who don't have that much money to lend would be a waste of time; they are not ***ABLE*** to lend you that amount of money.

You may believe you should try to "cozy up" to rich people, present them with a brilliant business plan, put together slide shows or dazzling sales pitches. Even though these people don't know you, you are sure that this proposition has enough merit that they will believe in your idea enough to make a worthwhile investment.

With your sales presentations, slide shows, value propositions and elevator pitches firmly in-hand, you set out to visit with the first rich person we can find. Confidently, you greet this stranger and then proceed right into conveying your practiced sales pitch. We entice them for the first 10 seconds with a scripted introduction. The rich person listens intently for the first 10 seconds (all while wondering… who are you and why are you here?) until you get to the part of your presentation asking them to loan you $10,000.

With a quizzical look, the person quickly says they are not interested. It even appeared for a split second the person found your proposition attractive. You wonder is disbelief, "How can this be possible?" I have a great message, and they are ABLE to lend me the money… what could have gone wrong?

Your keen business sense tells you to not stop with the first no, and so you press on to the next affluent person on the list. In a desperate effort to make this interaction better than the last one, you change up your slide show and a few words in the introduction. With confidence, you're lucky enough to land another meeting with this busy, successful person (by the way, securing a meeting is half the battle in the approach being discussed right now—the HSE Process teaches how to go about it the right way). You do your sales pitch all over again. While the person with money listens for a short period of time, once again he/she refuses and closes the door on the opportunity.

For the next week, you spend 40 hours making presentations to strangers on your list and make no progress. You begin to question the value of your business proposal. Is it really as good as you thought it was? You question your presentation skills and value in the world. By the end of the week you begin to conclude that "times are tough" and now is just not the right time for anyone to invest. In other words, you say to yourself, "There are no jobs out there because that's what the newspapers are saying."

After your hard week you decide to have dinner with your best friend from high school. You have been friends forever and would do anything for one other. You have been through good times and bad and have even helped each other out of tough jams. Some people even call you "twins from different mothers" because you see the world in the same way.

Your best friend asks, "Hey, can you spring for dinner tonight? I don't have a penny to my name until payday." You know that your friend is not really good with money and spends it as fast as they earn it. Even though they would be WILLING to, there is no way in the world that they would be ABLE to lend you the money you need. The two of you start discussing your past week, and you share how the meetings went concerning your business idea.

You describe to your broke friend that you just don't understand why you're not making any progress. You have a great business idea and these people clearly are ABLE to lend you the money… it has been so frustrating. You say out loud, "Anyone who knows me understands that I would never ask for a loan unless the idea was solid." (Of course, none of the people you met with actually knew you).

Your friend asks, "Well, I know you. Why didn't you ever come to me with this idea?" Sheepishly, you explain that you know he doesn't have that type of money. You further disclose that while the two of you would do anything for each other, you didn't want to put them on the spot because of their financial situation. They wouldn't be ABLE to lend you the money.

"What's wrong with you?" they respond. "Of course I don't have that type of money, but my uncle is part of an angel investing group and they look at deals much bigger than this every day!" You reply, "You would be WILLING to introduce me to your uncle?" "Don't be silly," your friend explains. "We are very close and he has always given me great advice. He has even told me that if I ever ran across a good idea worth investing in that I should tell him about it right away. Besides, you are my best friend in the world. I may not have the money, but I am WILLING to put my reputation on the line in front of my uncle."

A week later you are in front of your friend's uncle making your sales pitch. The uncle seems interested, but a little unsure about your idea. Your friend steps up and tells him about your personal and professional friendship. They even inform him about the great business ideas you've come up with in the past. His uncle agrees to let you present in front of his angel investor group.

The big day arrives and you are ready to present in front of this group of successful investors… now these people are definitely ABLE to lend you the money! You are confident of your success right until you enter the boardroom. To your complete horror, six of the people sitting on the angel investor group are the strangers that you presented to during your first week of door knocking! Your heart sinks. They have already turned me down face to face and now I'm about to be shot down again! As you begin presenting your great idea you feel doomed.

"Aren't you that young man who knocked on my door a few weeks ago?" one of them asks. "Yes sir, I am," you reply. "Didn't I tell you then that I wasn't in favor of your idea?" the same man asks. "I don't know you. How do I know that you really have credible ideas worth investing in?"

Before you can respond, your friend's uncle steps in. "My nephew has known this young man his whole life. He says he's had dozens of great business ideas over the years that have been funded and successful; I say we hear him out."

Ironically, 90 minutes later you are being patted on the back by some of the same people who knocked down your idea just a week or two earlier. You stand stunned in disbelief while holding a $10,000 check in your hand. How could this be? I had the same idea for the same amount of money that involved some of the same people. What happened?

Your friend's uncle takes you aside to congratulate you. You ask him that very same question, "What changed?" With a wry smile the uncle replies, "You made the first and biggest mistake last week. You focused on people that were ABLE to help you on your project, but they were not WILLING to help you. My nephew, on the other hand, was extremely WILLING to help you and he vouched for you as a genuine person with sound business ideas."

The uncle continues, "To be honest with you, had you knocked on my door a week ago I would have said no to your proposal as well. I didn't trust you when I agreed to help you; I trust my nephew and his judgment of you. I knew full well that he was putting his personal and professional reputation on the line when he brought you to me. If you were good enough for him to trust, you were good enough for me."

The message is clear and can be summarized by this simple phrase:

> ## "You can't push your way into an organization…you have to be invited."

You have two choices in job search:

1. **Bang on the door of an organization that you have not been invited into.**

2. **Let other people introduce you while providing credibility for you as a person and as a talented employee.**

The smart jobseeker realizes that #2 is the only reasonable direction to go-and it is something that they have already done many times in their life.

Willing & Able Come Together in HSE Networking

As you might guess after reading the story, the HSE way of networking focuses 95% of your time interacting with people who are WILLING to help you.

Those are the people who will get you in front of others who are ABLE to help you.

The traditional way of jumping right to people who are ABLE to help you may seem somewhat efficient on the surface, but it is not effective in the long run and how has that worked for you so far in your search?

Remember, we are networking by creating business relationships with people. When is the last time you achieved a meaningful relationship with anyone by being forceful and efficient ("I'd like you to be my friend and you have 20 seconds to decide")? All meaningful relationships in your personal or business life have been formed by making a connection with the person - and it usually involves an introduction from someone both of you already know.

In the HSE Process, you control your ability to connect with people and enable them to decide to help you. Everything you do from this point on will help guide people who are WILLING to help you get to individuals who are ABLE to help you.

> ## Marketing: You have to become interesting before you can become important

We just concluded an important learning objective. The old way of networking vs. *Human Search Engine* networking is significantly different. Also, remember from the previous chapter that every jobseeker has two problems they must solve in order to land a rewarding new role:

> *1. Nobody knows you exist—a company can't hire you until it knows you exist.*
>
> *2. You are unaware of at least 85% of the organizations that could use you.*

What I am teaching you is already a part of your daily life. That's why the HSE Process is so different. This is no newfangled infomercial way to do your job search. The HSE Process teaches you to do your search using skills you already have. The HSE Process guides you to use the experience you have from your own life and create a research project that leads you to a predictable result.

Most job search books spend a great deal of time recommending that you focus on resumes, cover letters and portfolios. I totally disagree! Why? Look at your own life for clues.

Look around you. How do products and services get sold? How do you decide to buy things and what influences your decisions? After just a few moments of watching TV or being online, the answer comes to you very quickly… marketing.

Unmistakable jingles and taglines create lasting messages. It is clear that nothing in this country is bought or sold without a planned and sustained marketing effort. If marketing is a good strategy for billion dollar international companies, I'm pretty sure it's relevant for jobseekers as well.

In order to market any product (in this case, your skills and abilities) we need to have a story to tell. Commercials sell products because their message connects with people. Your HSE marketing effort will be no different.

Relationships of any kind form slowly over time and begin with a simple introduction and finding of common interests. Your job search marketing will follow those same rules and consist of three levels of conversation as you introduce yourself to people who don't currently know you:

1. **Tagline**
2. **Focus Statement**
3. **60-Second Introduction**

These three messages will carry you from the initial introduction (Tagline) to creation of interest in a conversation (Focus Statement) all the way through describing your technical skills and target role (60-Second Introduction). It just makes sense to design your introduction and generation of interest with someone the same way that you have done it in your personal life.

If this is the way that you create relationships in your own life, then using that proven method in a systematic way makes a lot of sense. So let's begin creating your HSE messages…

> *An example of marketing the HSE way - What makes you different and worth talking to?*

Suppose for a moment you were working as a salesperson in charge of selling what you believe is the world's best hammer. This hammer you are promoting is truly unique and unlike any hammer people have ever seen before because it will drive any nail with one strike and it will never hit your finger (Just like your unique skills and experience make you different from other jobseekers that look the same at first glance). The hammer's special traits appear to be useful to a number of different industries and in a dozen different ways for each of those industries.

You are certain that if you could only get this hammer in front of people who would value its unique qualities, they would buy it and recommend the product to others in the industry. How in the world do you get the word out about this hammer?

You really have two problems in determining how to promote this amazing hammer:

 Even though this hammer appears on the surface to look like every other hammer on the market, how do you get people to see how special it really is? Can you articulate what is unique and beneficial about it?

 How do you determine which people and industries value the unique capabilities of this hammer? Once you identify them, how do you get in front of them?

If these two questions were effectively addressed, you could sell a lot of hammers! The process of answering these two questions is exactly what the HSE Process is all about. It should come as no surprise, that in this case, YOU are the unique and special hammer. That's right, you are going to do this research and promote yourself the same way that people have promoted tools and cans of tomato soup for 100 years… but it this case, you and your skill set are the item being marketed.

Here's a way to summarize the hammer example as if it related to you in your current job search situation. In these steps, the hammer is you.

Identify the unique characteristics of the hammer
Identify who values those unique characteristics
Uncover new markets of hammer buyers that are not obvious to the average salesperson because he or she is not using the HSE Process
Actively promote to those new markets that need this special hammer
Utilize contacts you already have in the hardware and building industries find opportunities to promote this hammer in person to people who value and buy hammers

Now you're inching closer to solving the two problems that every jobseeker has: no one knows you exist, and you're unaware of 85% of organizations that would value your skills.

Once you solve these two problems, a job is not far away. It's time to begin forming the message you will use in your conversations with people who value your skills and abilities.

Creating relationships is always done the same way…

Every relationship you have created in your life, personal or professional, was created first by a short introductory conversation that sought common ground (How about that weather? How about the

#1

Your Tagline

Packers?), then turned into a conversation to find similar beliefs or values (I'm a Republican/Democrat, I am passionate about airplanes) and finally move toward a detailed explanation of your background, skills, vocation or family status. If that has been true for every relationship you have created in your life so far why would creating relationships in your job search be any different? It isn't. That's why you need to develop messages for each step of the conversations you are about to have. This will help you seamlessly move from one stage of the relationship-building process to the next.

Taglines are not new and you are surrounded by them. These short 5-10 word phrases are designed to catch someone's attention create interest and invite questions. Are they important? When running for President of the United States, candidates start with a memorable Tagline. "Are you better off today than you were four years ago?" and "Read my lips…no new taxes" come to mind.

If the most powerful person in the world uses them in their job search— perhaps you should, too.

In the HSE process your tagline is defined as a phrase that is 5-7 words long, contains an oxymoron or non sequitur statement and generates questions. Your Tagline has one goal and one goal only… to get someone to ask **"What do you mean by that?"**

Think about it for a second. You can talk AT someone as long as you would like but **UNTIL THEY ASK YOU A QUESTION THEY ARE NOT REALLY INVOLVED IN THE CONVERSATION**. A question shows a desire to know more about your topic. It is the way people continue a conversation and it demonstrates interest. Getting someone to ask a question is really the only true sign that someone is invested in the conversation and looking for more.

The Tagline is like a catchy hook you use before giving a presentation or writing a persuasive article. **I like to think an effective Tagline will make a person spin around like a German shepherd hearing a high-pitched whistle.** Your goal is first to get the listener's attention, then answer questions from that person (because they want to learn more).

Similar to the idea that "You can't push your way into any organization; you have to be invited" a Tagline gives you the ability to get people to ask questions. This serves as an "invitation" to continue the conversation. Pushing your way into any new relationship is not a good idea. Jobseekers need to stop pushing their way into organizations.

Here is an example of an effective Tagline I have used for years as a career counselor, "A plan that takes the fear out of job search." How does this fit the criteria explained above? First, the word fear instantly catches someone's attention. Anyone who has ever looked for a new job knows the fear I am referring to. It's the fear of how long the money will last or of being judged by someone.

The non-sequitur in my Tagline is the combination of the words "plan" and "job search" used together in the same sentence. Most people cannot conceive the idea that you have enough control over your search to make a plan. Even if someone knows this, how would he or she know it's a useful plan and how to execute it?

Initial reactions to my Tagline almost always make people say, "Tell me more about that" or something like it. That's the whole goal, isn't it? The final result of what started as your Tagline could be an extension of immediate dialogue or a face-to-face, one-hour informal meeting or an actual interview! The beginning point, however, is an initial connection that gets them to want to learn more about you.

Here are some other samples of good Taglines:

Creating a brand without saying a word (for marketing professionals)

The pain-free dentist

An IT professional who speaks English

An attorney who stays out of court

An administrative professional who can create order out of chaos

Now, write your own Tagline on the worksheet in the following pages and test it on a few people who you know. Does it get them to ask questions? Remember, the Tagline doesn't tell the whole story; it simply gets other people interested enough to ask you for more information. At this time, let's explore how to optimize the use of a Tagline.

When you meet someone new and the person asks what you do for a living, give them your Tagline. I understand that type of question (What you do for a living?) can be hard to answer for someone who is unemployed. Practice it for a while as a ready response. Then, try your Tagline on a few people who you know personally (WILLING), but who you don't know on a professional basis (UNABLE).

See how they react. You may have to adjust your response along the way based on certain personalities—perhaps modify your nonverbal communication or tone when stating the Tagline. Don't be cute with your Tagline though…puns are fine, but don't go overboard. The only good Tagline is the one that gets people to ask, "What do you mean by that?" That question is an open invitation to a conversation. Remember, you can't push your way into a conversation—you have to be invited.

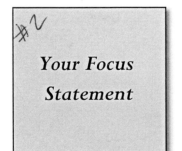

Your Focus Statement

Finally, start using your Tagline as a branding statement during job search. List it on your job search business cards (yes, you need business cards for your job search—how will people know how to contact you?) and lead with it at networking events and job fairs. Businesses spend billions being known by only a few words, so let's follow their lead.

There is an old saying: "Nobody cares how much you know until they know how much you care." Think about that for a moment. You've been taught to conduct a job search by dazzling people with your technical and people skills, and there is a time for that (coming next in the 60-Second Introduction).

Again, think of every new relationship (personal or business) you have formed in your life. After you say hello to a person (your Tagline), what is the next thing that the two of you do? You find common ground to discuss. Often you will talk about the weather, an event, a sports contest, a TV show, work, etc.

When you use the HSE Process, your goal is to choreograph the first moments of every new conversation you engage in. You know there will be an awkward silence about 15 seconds into the conversation (like there has been in your conversations with every new person you've met and will meet).

This is where your Focus Statement comes in

The goal of the Focus Statement is simple, but very hard for some to understand because it contains no work history, no achievements, no education and no tangible results. This runs contrary to how most people want introduce themselves during a job search. You have been taught to impress people with your accomplishments in hopes they roll out the red carpet for you. Has that ever really happened in any relationship in your life?

Look at a typical conversation with any new person you meet. You introduce yourself and engage in a brief discussion about what both of you do for a living (wow, that Tagline could sure come in handy here). After you nod in acknowledgement of that information, the silence drives you to try another mutual topic of interest. You will talk about where you live, where you grew up, where you went to school… all in a very emotionless exchange of facts that neither person can really expound on. Then you hit on something that you both feel strongly about and the conversation changes immediately. It may be politics, sports, volunteering, a local referendum, etc., anything where a shared passion comes into play.

If you try to impress a person you just met, they will quickly ask where the restroom is or excuse themselves to grab a coffee—only not to return. If the two of you don't find some common ground, the conversation ends quickly.

If that is true with the hundreds of people you have met in your own life, it's probably true in networking relationships? Networking relationships ARE just like any other relationship in your life – they are real, important and require time and nurturing. Remember, "Nobody cares how much you know until they know how much you care." No young man looking to introduce himself to a young lady starts the conversation with his achievements, education, or technical description of who they are. Can you imagine that conversation?

"Hi, my name's Ben and I'm 6' 1" and weigh 195 pounds. I'm a graduate of a prestigious university and have very good teeth. I make $50,000 a year as an accountant, but my parents have a lot of money and I stand to inherit it someday. Would you like to go out with me?"

Wow. Ask any young lady to read that last paragraph and then ask her what she thinks of that type of intro. You wouldn't use that kind of introduction in your own life, so why would you believe it would work in networking for job? Remember, I'm talking about networking, not a conversation with a hiring manager for an open position. With a hiring manager in an interview, your achievements are certainly going to be part of the conversation, but in the case of meeting new people to create relationships, lead with passion.

> **The passion you need in that conversation is in your Focus Statement.**

Focus Statements are about passion for the work you do. That's it! In the next part of your introduction (the 60-Second Intro), I promise you will get every chance to unveil all of your achievements, skills and philosophies. For now, focus on letting others know why you decided to become a dentist instead of a circus clown. What is it about being an engineer that makes you leap out of bed every day? Is there something from your childhood experience that made you want to be a teacher since the age of 10? Did someone impact your life in a really positive way, and now you want to do the same kind of work that that person did because of that influence?

There is usually some seminal moment when you decided to do the kind of work that you do. Perhaps your father was an accountant, and you saw it provided a good, steady life for his family. Furthermore, his career allowed your mom to stay home with you (or maybe your mom was the accountant and dad stayed home). Did a police officer or firefighter influence your life in a positive way and you became drawn to one of these professions? Where you naturally mechanical as a child and drove your parents' crazy tearing things apart because you just had to know how they worked? Did a doctor or nurse play a critical role in your family's life? Was there a teacher who influenced you early in your educational career? Was there a TV show that piqued your interest in doing the work you do now? Have you always had an innate desire to help people?

The HSE Focus Statement is about your passion and drive to do the type of work that you are seeking in your next role. It is the brief, 20-30 second story you share with someone when discussing your job search. Subsequently, the Focus Statement gives this person an idea of your industry of interest. Make no mistake about it people will only refer you to their personal and professional acquaintances if they are convinced your integrity and passion for doing this work is evident.

Remember, people put their reputation on the line every time they make a referral. So why is passion for your work so important to express in the first few minutes you meet someone? What does being passionate about your work guarantee this other person?

I must answer the two preceding questions with a question to provoke some important thought here. What do we know for sure about passionate people in our lives? Think for a second about the three or four people in your life you know are truly passionate about what they do. Picture them in your mind. What do they look like? What do they sound like? How hard do they work to improve themselves for the greater good of their work and the people around them?

The point here is what makes a "good employee?" *If you were to refer them to one of your personal or professional friends, how sure are you they will represent you well?* That's the question that matters in the discussion about whether people will refer you to others during your search.

Remember: *Be humble, be sincere and ask for help. Your passion about whatever work you do is the best way to exemplify "being sincere". You should light up when you share your Focus Statement. It should be apparent to everyone around you that this topic and this work excites you.* **When you deliver your Focus Statement, you should have a look on your face like a 5-year old talking about Santa Claus!**

Focus Statement Parameters and Sample

Here are the parameters of your Focus Statement:

1. **It should only last 20-30 seconds**
2. **It should be in a story format that "paints a picture"**
3. **You should deliver it with genuine passion (without going overboard, of course)**
4. **Your experiences that led you to your line of work must resonate clearly as a conclusion**

As a point of reference, here is my own Focus Statement:

"When it comes to job search, I have made every mistake a person can make. I've chosen a career based on a TV show, run scared to an industry that I would never have chosen for myself, spent 20 years in leadership positions in an industry I couldn't have cared less about, chased money, worked for incompetent and evil bosses, and then out of desperation and lucky timing, learned an incredible new way to look for a job that made perfect sense, but I had never heard of it. My goal in teaching this job search process is to let people learn from my mistakes and empower them to take control of their lives."

Do you have a picture in your mind right now? Do you have questions for me? Does my passion for this work make sense to you? Are you interested in learning more?

Good Focus Statements pull people into a conversation and cause them to invite you further in. From there, the dialogue generates even more interest. **You have become interesting, now you can become important.**

Now, write your Focus Statement. Dig deep and forget about impressing people. Focus on engaging them. Test it on people who you know personally, but not professionally. If it draws them into the conversation, you now have their attention enough to start talking about your qualifications, experiences, and achievements... enter your **60-Second Introduction**.

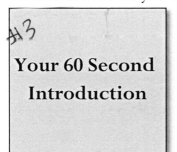

Your 60 Second Introduction

This is the point when most HSE jobseekers tuck away their desire to proclaim, "I need to tell people how great I am that they will be so impressed they'll hire me!" If that's the case for you, it is validation that you have learned one HUGE lesson.

While you will definitely be using some of your skills and accomplishments as part of your introduction, you will be melding those elements with a continued attempt to *sincerely connect* with the person you are talking to.

Remember, "You can't push your way into any organization or relationship... you have to be invited." The 60-Second Introduction is your chance to build credibility with a person while maintaining interest in your story.

In the HSE Process, there are five parts to a 60-Second Introduction:

1.	Restate your name and give people a way to remember it
2.	Describe what you are looking for in your next position in terms of duties, level, responsibilities and industry (the goal here is to paint a picture of where someone has seen that type of job before so you are discussing the same type of job). Don't just use a job title. Remember, there are managers of local convenience stores (with all due respect) and there are managers of divisions of multi-national organizations.
3.	Provide a brief work history (20 seconds or less and make sure you demonstrate a logical transition from your previous positions to the role you are looking for).
4.	Describe an achievement you are proud of and/or brought value to an organization (make sure this accomplishment is measurable and demonstrates the skills you are claiming to possess).
5.	Offer a work-related tidbit that helps set the stage for the small talk that inevitably ensues after your introduction is complete (We know the two of you will be searching for something to discuss after you stop talking. Instead of hoping that the topic will show you in a positive light, let's make sure it does by "priming the pump").

A sample 60-Second Introduction:

"Hi, my name is Chris Czarnik—that's *Czar* like Czar of Russia and *Nik* like Nicolas."
"What I'm looking for in my next position is an opportunity to speak in front of large audiences on the topics of career choices and job search. This would be at college campuses or in Workforce Development organizations. I would also be creating job search curriculum and training others to teach the HSE job search process."
"My work experience includes more than 20 years of leadership roles, including the military and industry with a heavy concentration on HR and hiring manager responsibilities. For the past decade, I have been teaching professional job search to more than 300 individual executive clients while working for a national career search firm. Four years ago, I started my own company and have been traveling the Midwest speaking at high schools, colleges and universities on the topics of career choice and job search."
"I am proud to say that in 2005 I was recognized as an outstanding career advisor for a national career search firm, and in 2008 was contracted by the University of Wisconsin-Madison, a Division 1 University of more than 45,000 students, to write the career search curriculum for a high profile department of the college. I now teach that job search curriculum to the athletic department as a guest instructor several times a semester."
"One of the most interesting things about working with the university's athletic department is that the football and basketball players you watch on ESPN on Saturday are in my classroom on Tuesday."

Think of the last part… number 5—the interesting work-related tidbit of information. What questions do you think surface after I finish delivering that statement? They run the gamut. Are the players really that strong (or fast)?" "How do they get their homework done with all that traveling?"

Regardless of what questions the person asks, we will be talking about one of the things that I am most proud of in my career… working at the University of Wisconsin-Madison, a very prestigious Big Ten university. It is virtually impossible for the first five minutes of the conversation to be dull or uninteresting… and how long does it take for a person to decide if he or she will connect with me? You guessed it… less than five minutes.

> **Here are your next assignments**

Write your Tagline, Focus Statement and 60-Second Introduction. Try them first on people you know really well *personally, but not professionally*. See if they think it is a good reflection of who you really are. You may need to revise these conversational tools several times during the HSE Process as you get feedback.

After you refine these three tools, test them on people who you know professionally—in other words, folks who have a good feel for your skill set. These are people you have worked with in the past. Do they think it's an accurate professional representation of you? Does it make them want to ask questions?

How will you know when you've got it right? Well, as people say, you'll just know. When you get the intended reactions and questions, you'll just know. When you deliver it with confidence and vigor, you'll just know. When people are anxious to learn more about you, you'll just know. Keep refining it and collecting feedback from others who want to help you. When will you be ready for the next step, which is doing informational interviews and networking meetings? You guessed it, you'll just know.

Writing Your Tagline

Your tagline is a phrase that is 5-7 words long. It has one goal and one goal only—to get someone to ask: **"What do you mean by that?"** Your tagline piques someone's interest and opens up the conversation.

To write your tagline, consider the following...

1. What is your industry, position title or primary responsibility? **Hint: Avoid jargon! The goal is to be relatable and interesting.**

2. What makes you different, unique or unexpected? **This is typically your oxymoron or non-sequitor statement.**

Now put it all together in a concise, compelling 5-7 word phrase. Remember, your goal is to invite the question: "What do you mean by that?" **Until they ask you a question, they are not really involved in the conversation**

Download a PDF version of this worksheet at www.myhumansearchengine.com

Crafting Your Focus Statement

Focus Statements are about passion for the work you do. **They contain no work history, no achievements, no education, and no tangible results**. Your Focus Statement is about what drives you to do the type of work you love.

You should **light up** when you give your Focus Statement. It should be apparent to everyone around you that this topic and this work **excites** you. In developing your Focus Statement, consider the following:

1. How did you get here? **What experiences led you to this line of work? What missteps did you make? What lessons did you learn along the way?**

2. Why does what you do matter? **What impact do you make through your work? How do you make a difference to your community, company, coworkers, etc.?**

Now put it all together in **a 20-30 second** short story format. Remember: Your Focus Statement should paint a picture for the listener. It should be uniquely personal so that it doesn't apply to anyone else, and it should be delivered with genuine passion and enthusiasm. Dig deep and forget about impressing people. Focus on engaging them!

Download a PDF version of this worksheet at www.myhumansearchengine.com

Developing Your 60-Second Introduction

The 60-Second Introduction is your chance to **build credibility** with a person while maintaining interest in your story. It should contain the following five elements:

1. Restate your name and give people a way to remember it.

2. Describe what you are looking for in your next position in terms of duties, level, responsibilities, and industry. **Hint: Don't just use a job title!**

3. Provide a brief work history in 20 seconds or less. **Make sure you demonstrate a logical transition from your previous positions to the job you want to land next.**

4. Describe an achievement that you are proud of and/or brought value to an organization. **This should be measurable and clearly demonstrate the skills you are claiming to possess.**

5. Offer an interesting work-related tidbit that helps set the stage for small talk after your introduction is complete.

Download a PDF version of this worksheet at www.myhumansearchengine.com.

CHAPTER 9: HOW AND WHY HSE WORKS

Over a decade of experience with thousands of people

Until now, this book has been about sharing insight on why traditional job search methods fail, the job search perspective from the hiring or HR manager's side of the desk, and a step-by-step method to preparing and presenting yourself in a well-planned way that helps you land your next role. You've become aware of your unique personality, background and skills, as well as what it takes to network as a means of meeting specific goals. You might be asking yourself, "OK, Chris, this is all good stuff, but what do I need to do to put the HSE Process into action?" That's what I'll share with you next.

Once again, remember—the HSE Process solves the two biggest problems in job search: 1) Nobody knows you exist and 2) You are currently unaware of 85% of the organizations that could hire you. In simple terms, you lack two things: **information** and **exposure**. You are going to fix both of those issues by creating opportunities to be in front of people. Using old methods, that is why you sent out all of those cover letters and resumes, right? The goal of sending all of those documents was to get an opportunity to have face-to-face conversations in your industry of interest, wasn't it?

The HSE Process creates face-to-face opportunities *outside* of the normal hiring process. That's right, if done correctly, your search will avoid the HR department of an organization altogether until someone from inside the company brings you there for an introduction.

Remember, you can't push your way into an organization; you have to be invited. Sending resumes and cover letters to a complete stranger at an organization and expecting to end up the number one choice out of 100 people who applied is a bit of a pipe dream. You are pounding on the door of a party you're not invited to. Your goal is to have someone from inside the organization open the door to that party for you.

Let's be clear; I have nothing against HR departments. Heck, I used to work in one! HR professionals are fine human beings who got into that line of work because they genuinely like people. They are doing the best they can using current hiring processes. Until organizations change their mindset and undergo a complete paradigm shift in hiring, HR professionals must continue to work within an inefficient and ineffective system of finding talent. The problem is the system is designed to eliminate you as a candidate for the position, not choose you.

In fact, in a hiring situation where there are 100 applicants for one job, HR's core function is to systematically eliminate 99% of the applicants. That's not my theory. In many cases, their first job is not to find the right person; it is to eliminate the wrong people! Intentionally, the process is to find fault in your application or resume so they can eliminate you as a candidate.

Again, it's not their fault. This process involves sifting through countless candidates in order to perform 15 phone screens and 7 first interviews. The truth is that in most cases the hiring process is about reaching a manageable number of strong candidates as quickly and systemically as possible, and yes, for the most part, all off of a piece of paper.

That's right, you as a candidate spent hours writing and revising your resume and cover letter specifically for that job, applied for the position with great enthusiasm and anticipation, and the first duty of the person who receives it is to find a reason to put it in the "NO" pile. Again, don't be upset with HR people; it's the process.

Before you become more frustrated, ask yourself a different question, "What was the goal of sending the resume and cover letter in the first place?" Did you expect a job offer as a result sending it off into the black hole of cyber space?

No! You sent in the resume and cover letter hoping someone seeing your information would invite you in for a face-to-face conversation (or at least a phone interview). If that is the goal, then the following concept is critical for you to understand.

The HSE method of job search focuses on creating face-to-face meetings with hiring managers in a different way. If I told you there was some secret handshake or magical password that could get you hired, you would be skeptical, as expected. Your progress using the HSE Process will be measured by your ability to get in front of people who can help you on your search (which you are in complete control of). This sure beats being screened out by some computer program because your resume lacked a word or two.

If I've heard it once, I've heard it a thousand times from jobseekers: "If I could only get in front of the people who have the problems I can solve, I know I could really impress them. The problem is I can't get anyone from that organization to talk to me!" Due to conventional hiring processes, great candidates sit at home with a rejection letter while hiring managers ask, "Where's all the talent?" The irony is hiring managers know there is talent somewhere, but how do they find it? The HSE Process makes you easy to find for the people who have the problems that your skills will solve.

This connection will not happen accidently. You need to help create the circumstances that allow this connection to occur. You will have informational interviews and networking meetings so you meet the person who needs you long before they have a job opening. Since you can't push your way into an organization, you need to be the answer to their problems by creating opportunities to be in the right place at the right time.

Before I close this chapter, I want to cement into your mind the idea that what I am teaching you is something you have experienced many times in your life. That's right! The difference is these prior occurrences always happened by accident. Now you are going to make them happen on purpose.

Almost everyone has had a great restaurant referred to them by a friend or neighbor. "Wow, have you tried the pizza at Luigi's? It's fantastic! You and I like the same type of pizza, and I'm telling you it is great! You've got to go there." What happens next is predictable. You do not scan the ingredients list at Luigi's. You don't do a price comparison between them and all of the other local pizza joints. You go to Luigi's simply based on the recommendation of your fellow pizza-loving friend. Great end result, but did you do anything to make that end result happen? What if you really needed to find a great pizza place but just waited around for someone to recommend one?

In the case of waiting for a recommendation, you don't mention to anyone that you need to find a great pizza place, because you are just sure that if a person knew of one, he or she would initiate this **specific conversation**. You stand there surrounded by pizza aficionados, but nothing is said to you because they have no idea that you need their advice. You become increasingly frustrated with your friends because no one is helping you!

Finally, you get frustrated with them for not recommending a place to you (even though you never asked) and go visit a random pizza place on your own. Unfortunately, the pizza and the service there are not that good. You conclude that there are no good pizza places in town, because if there were, somebody would have told you about them. I mean, they are your friends after all. At the same time a strange thing is going on. A friend hears that you went to a below-average pizza place and wonders why you chose that restaurant! If asked, he would have been happy to give you advice on another. So, what went wrong here?

This story goes a long way to explain why networking often fails, especially when it comes to job search. People randomly apply to organizations they have never heard of and get nowhere. If they do ask friends for help with their search, typically it is done like this: "If any of you know of any jobs out there, or if you can get me in where you work that would be great (the equivalent of asking them to drive you to the pizza place, buy your pizza for you and clean up your mess)." Job seekers don't do that because they think it will work well, but because they have no idea what else to do. Until now.

You need people's ***advice, guidance and feedback***, then you can take it from there. You cannot cross your fingers and hope that conversations or advice appear out of the blue. You need to initiate conversations and ask people for guidance that will help you. As I say all of the time, "People want to help you with your job search but they don't know how. You need to teach them how. Proactive job search means exactly that. Using the HSE Process, you don't wait for things to happen; you make them happen."

The last example I will share before teaching you how to make these conversations happen gets the same response in every city I speak in. The first time I used it I wasn't certain it would make the connection I was hoping for, but the response I got told me everything I needed to know. I ask the ladies in the audience how they chose their OB-GYN.

The decision of which OB-GYN to choose is clearly far more important to ladies than men could ever imagine. The idea of choosing one <u>without a referral</u> is met with incredulous looks from virtually every woman in the room. There is no way they would ever just choose someone out of the yellow pages and cross their fingers and hope that it's a good choice! This decision is far too important to leave to chance! From state to state, I hear the same response—women don't wait for a recommendation to find their OB-GYN; they actively solicit advice from other women.

While I can't speak about the woman-doctor relationship from first-hand knowledge, I think it's fair to say where you end up working 2,000 hours a year is also a pretty big decision. This is a decision that requires information, advice and feedback from other people who know more about these companies or industries than you do.

A leaky pipe and an answer at your door– Why HSE makes hiring manager's lives easier

I've tried at some length to describe why the HSE Process works in your favor, but what really matters is why companies love to use this process to find new employees. The easiest way to describe it (which I've stated before) is that you are going to ***"put a ham sandwich in front of a hungry person and see if they want to eat it. If they don't want to eat it you are going to ask them to refer you to another hungry person that they know."***

We've already established that in a perfect world companies would not need to receive 100 resumes for every job ad, perform 15 phone screens, 7 first interviews and 3 second interviews and at the end hire a complete stranger. No, in a perfect world the obvious answer to their problems would show up right in front of them just as they were realizing they had a problem that needed to be fixed in their organization (or better yet, before they realized it). In essence, that is exactly what you are trying to do by using the HSE Process. Here is an example that makes the intent of the Process clear:

Let's say you are a person who normally takes the decision to hire a contractor for repairs on your home very seriously. Whether it is painting or drywall, plumbing or finishing a basement, you would never hire anyone without getting competitive bids from multiple prospects. You interview each of them and take a good deal of time with your decision to make sure you get the EXACT right person. With all the time in the world to make this decision and no immediate urgency to act you are painstaking in your research.

One morning, however, you wake up and hear a strange noise coming from your basement. As you descend the stairs you are horrified to see the main water pipe coming into your house has broken and 100 gallons of water per minute are flooding in. Frantically you start thinking about how to find someone to fix this urgent problem. Your mind starts reeling over the prospect of searching online or in the phone book to choose a plumber at random. What if they aren't qualified? Are they safe to bring into my home? How soon can they get there? Your mind spins with the negative possibilities of choosing someone at random. And then the doorbell rings.

As you open the door you are amazed to find a local plumber standing there, handing out flyers about the work he does. The flyer speaks specifically of emergency services and the repair of water mains in houses. This is too good to be true. Is the answer to your problem right in front of you EXACTLY when I need it? You are further amazed when the plumber says he has done work for two of your neighbors and you are welcome to call them for references.

While normally you would be asking for three price quotes before making a choice, at this moment your choice is clear. You ask the plumber to get his tools and get to work fixing your pipe. ***He will not compete with anyone for this job because he was the right person in the right place at the right time.***

The HSE Process will allow you to put yourself in front of organizations that likely have the problems you are uniquely able to solve. It will only take one of them with an immediate need to see you are the answer right on their doorstep!

Now let's talk about how YOU can be the plumber on the doorstep of the company that needs you.

CHAPTER 10: INFORMATIONAL INTERVIEWS & NETWORKING MEETINGS

Definitions and Explanations

There are two different types of meetings in the HSE Process: Informational Interviews and Networking Meetings. I will compare and contrast them before we discuss how to hold each of these meetings.

Informational Interviews: In general terms, you will conduct Informational Interviews with people who work in the world (industry) that you want to work in next. They have industry-specific knowledge you will need to know. They know people in the industry and understand the type of people the industry values. They are also aware of the problems that need to be solved in that industry. They are a direct connection to others in your targeted field of work.

Networking Meetings: People you meet in these meetings may or may not work in your field of expertise (the industry you want to work in next), but they are connectors, they "know people." Examples of these people might be bankers, lawyers, teachers, salespeople or consultants. These people may have no direct connection to your industry, but the nature of their work depends on knowing lots of people from all walks of life. Their connections are critical for success. You meet with them so they can introduce you to people who work in the world you want to work in. ***The only goal of a networking meeting is to be referred to someone with whom you can conduct an informational interview.***

Let's compare and contrast these two types of meetings:

Similarities

Each of these meetings has the following goals:

1. To introduce you to people who don't know you or to ones who do know you, but don't know how to help you with your job search.

2. To gain information and details that will help to advance your research efforts. This information might be industry details, names of additional contacts, definition of specific industry problems to be solved, names of organizations inside your desired career that you have never heard of, feedback on your job search presentation, and position descriptions in your field that you did not know existed.

3. To be considered and remembered in a positive light by leaving behind a great impression and the idea that you will be an asset to some organization (despite neither of you knowing where that is yet).

4. To specifically receive a referral (or two or three) _by name_ of someone the other person thinks would be important for you to speak with next to assist your research ("If you were me, who might be the best resource…"). _By name_ is a very important component here. If you don't get a direct referral, who do you call tomorrow morning to continue your research?

5. To gain specific advice, guidance and feedback from them (based on your conversation) about how to further your research.

Differences

1. Informational Interviews will focus on industry information that directly relates to your area of expertise. Networking Meetings will contain very little conversation about your industry or job type because the person with whom you are meeting isn't from that "world."

2. The results of Informational Interviews will lead you to research the organization or career field to identify specific industry needs or desires you can focus on as a way of **creating value** as a potential new employee. Networking Meetings are focused on people who can get you face-to- face conversations with others to help you with your search through connections.

3. Informational Interviews will most likely be held with people who are ABLE to help you. Networking Meetings will be held with people who are WILLING to help you.

4. Informational Interviews provide paths to do research and follow up. Networking Meetings will seem less direct, but involve teaching people who are WILLING to help you navigate you to those who are ABLE to help you.

5. The ONLY real goal of a networking meeting is to get a referral to someone in your industry or job type that you can have an informational interview with.

Why do we need two different kinds of meetings in the HSE Process? Both of these meetings answer one of two important questions:

Can I transition into a different type of work or a different industry with my skill set, education and experience?	How do I get back into the same job or industry that I was in during my last career?
In this case (Informational Interview), there are many questions to be answered. You have proven ability in the project management of a small, $5 million manufacturing firm. Could those same skills work for you in a large government organization? You have been a creative marketing design professional your whole career, but now you want to transition into a career in sales. Will a hiring manager see you as a viable candidate? You have been the executive director of a non-profit organization; will decision-makers at for-profit organizations consider you for their positions? The only way to receive insight to these questions is to talk with people who live and work in the type of organization you want to transition into.	In this case (Networking Meeting), you have the skills, education and experience needed to do the job because you demonstrated those traits in your last career. Now all you need is to find similar organizations that have the same types of problems to be solved like the last company you worked for. This meeting will focus on referrals to people who work in those types of organizations. You will focus on customers, competitors and vendors of your previous employer.

Think of the information you need to gather to make your transition into a new position like this: "What don't I know about making this transition, and who inside that type of organization could answer that question for me?" Forget entirely about trying to push your way into organizations until you answer this question and others like it through conversations with people who know the ins and outs of that industry. **Remember, first and foremost this is a research project and the topic of that research project is: "Who values my skills and abilities?"** Informational interviews are how you get the answers to that question.

Advice, Guidance and Feedback

It is about this point when I am teaching the HSE Process in a classroom that I see a few jobseekers view these meetings as "clever left-hand sells." Some individuals actually think it's time to drop off resumes to these important people instead of experiencing conversations with them. This is an _enormous_ mistake. You need to remember two things about the meetings you are about to have:

The people who hold high-level jobs in organizations know exactly what you are trying to accomplish using this method; they have used it most of their professional lives. You see, what I am teaching you is not new. This method of job search has been used by people at upper levels for well over a half of century. Think about it for a moment. Do you really think the president of a company looks in the Sunday newspaper job ads when he or she is in career transition? Look for yourself if you don't believe me. Visit any job site and look how many "president of company" jobs you find there. Board member jobs? CEO jobs? There are very few, so how do these people find their next position? Networking.

I will promise that the individuals you meet through the HSE Process can read people very well. That's how they got to where they are today. So, if you approach them for an "Informational Interview" and then try to turn it into a job interview with resume in-hand, they are going to be offended and recoil from helping you. You will never need to ask for a job if you are in a Networking Meeting with someone who **needs** you, it will occur to them that you should be talking about possibilities and opportunities in their own organization.

The goal of these meetings is to gain advice, guidance and feedback. Let's learn a little bit more about what I mean by advice, guidance and feedback.

Advice: Have you even genuinely been asked for advice from someone? How did you feel? Pretty great, right? They chose you of all people to get advice from which makes you feel as though they respect your opinion. They think of you as an expert on a topic and so you feel even better about the conversation. How long would you be willing to talk to this person if he or she truly wanted nothing from you except your advice? A long time I would guess…

Guidance: If you want guidance on your job search, who would be a good source? How about professionals who are now working but have been on a job search themselves the last two years? How WILLING do you think someone would be who has the emotions and experiences of job search fresh in his or her mind, to share some perspective? How did they go about their search? Who did they meet with? What did they learn along the way? What would this person do differently?

Feedback: Holding meetings with people close to you who are WILLING to help you produces honest feedback on your presentation style, your message and your job search strategy. What resonated with them about your presentation? What confused them? Was your message clear? Can they name a couple of organizations that fit the description of the kinds of places you want to work?

Here's one final lesson before you learn how to conduct Informational Interviews and Networking Meetings. At the end of any meeting, become comfortable asking this question of the person with whom you are meeting:

> **"Now that you know how I am going about my job search, if you were me (pause)—who would you want to talk to next to continue your research?" Another way of saying it is: "If you were me (pause)—what next steps would you take to drive your search forward?"**

After asking the question, stop talking and let them think. **Stay silent.** The ideas that these people will have for you are astounding! If you've followed the blueprint of connecting accordingly to these individuals, these ideas are going to amaze you.

The nuts and bolts of networking the HSE way

Once you have an opportunity to meet with someone for a Networking Meeting or Informational Interview, how long will the meeting last? Who will lead the meeting? How will you know if the meeting was effective? How do you ask for advice, guidance and feedback?

I'm about to script the questions to ask, word-for-word, and in the order in which you ask them for these meetings. But first, here are responses to the questions above to give you a solid organizational framework for this step in the HSE Process.

How long will these meetings last?	While you will ask for 20 minutes of his or her time (it's attractive because the number is less than a half hour), these meetings will often last 45 minutes to an hour. Check-in with the person with whom you are meeting at the 20-minute mark and ask permission to continue. This shows respect for the person's time.

If your meetings are only lasting 20 minutes, my guess is that you're not connecting with people, and you need to revisit how you are presenting yourself. I have had HSE clients who asked for 20-minute meetings and end up with one-to-three hour meetings, introductions to other leaders in the organization, plant tours and even invitations to complete applications that very day.

Who will lead these meetings?

Just like every other business meeting you have planned, you are in charge of this meeting. You requested the meeting; you are the one who knows what the desired outcomes are.

You will drive the meeting, ask the questions, keep it on schedule and reroute the conversation if it gets off topic. Remember, if you want to present yourself as a professional, then running a focused meeting is a great way to demonstrate your professionalism from the get-go.

Yes, this is another intentional strategy of the HSE Process that puts you in the limelight! It is a subtle, yet demonstrative way to create a great first impression and showcase the unique you! If you have not run many meetings (or any meetings), the beauty of the HSE Process is that it is designed for you get a lot of practice within your network of people before ever speaking with someone new.

How will you know if the meeting was effective?

This is actually very easy to determine. If the person with whom you meet provides a referral **BY NAME** and offers to connect you with this contact, then you know you're on the right track.

Don't forget another important end result - the person may suggest industries or companies that you should consider in alignment with the types of organizations you want to learn more about.

Asking for advice, guidance and feedback during the meeting

Here is where we cover the exact questions to ask during your meeting. It is important to use these questions as stated and in the order they are positioned.

After a few meetings, you may modify these questions a bit based on feedback that you receive. Starting out, however, use this script to take the nervousness out of your initial meetings.

Anticipating the needs of the people you meet with

Before we start discussing exactly how to conduct a networking meeting or informational interview it is important to consider the perspective of the person that you are going to meet with. What are they thinking? If we can identify how to lead them through a logical progression from the start of the meeting to the end we can make sure that we lead the meeting in a way that makes them comfortable and makes them ABLE to help us. What questions are going through their minds as the meeting begins?

Here is how I think it goes in their mind:

During the first three minutes of the meeting

Who are you?

Why are you here?

Do we have similar backgrounds or know similar people?

Are you who you say you are?

If you are successful answering those concerns, their next thoughts will be…

During minutes 3-15

What are you good at?

Can you prove with examples that you have these skills?

What are you looking for in your next opportunity?

Are you truly interested in my advice and guidance?

And if we get to this part they begin to wonder how they can help…

Minutes 15 through the end of the meeting

Who do I know who has similar experiences or background?

What types of problems are you uniquely able to solve?

Am I comfortable introducing you to my friends?

Where do you fit in the word of work?

What types of organizations fit the description of what you are looking for?

Now that you understand their thought process, let's discuss EXACTLY how to hold each of these meetings.

CHAPTER 11: INFORMATIONAL INTERVIEW SCRIPTS

How-to Conduct an Informational Interview

1. Thank the interviewee by NAME for meeting with you and give your **Focus Statement** and your **60-Second Introduction**

2. *Can you give me an idea of what is going on in the industry right now?* The goal is to get the person talking by asking about something he or she deals with every day. This also helps you uncover problems that need to be solved in this respective industry.

3. *How did you, _____, (use the person's NAME) get involved in this industry?* This question makes it easy for the person to continue a conversation. The interviewee is discussing a topic no one knows better than he or she does! Here you may find common ground to navigate the rest of the conversation and perhaps learn pathways into that industry.

4. *What skill sets are important for someone looking to be successful this industry?* This is the first moment that you will begin interjecting examples of your skill sets into the conversation. Remember, give enough information to let them know why you are going to be a great employee for an organization.

   For example, if the interviewee says problem solving is a good trait to have as a project manager, reply as follows, "Well, I'm glad to hear you say that. In my last two positions, analytical problem solving was a big part of my role as a project manager (or whatever title you held—but again, the emphasis here is on skill). Let me give you an example of how we solved a particular problem in my last role (bring this skill to life with a clear, but brief example with clear positive results).

5. *What kind of person succeeds in this industry?* The answer to this question will help you understand the personal traits of a person who fits well in the industry. Now demonstrate those traits with real life examples—again be succinct.

6. *What do I need to be aware of during my search—do you have any advice for me as I continue my search?* People love to give advice. If the interviewee sincerely thinks you will use his or her advice, the conversation becomes even more productive. The person may talk about his or her last job search. *Then, ask if they believe that networking is the right way to go about your search.* If the response is "yes," the next question will be hard for the interviewee to ignore.

7. *I have a great deal more research to do before making a choice of organizations or an industry. The best way you can help me today is by connecting me with other people who would be helpful in my search. If you were me, who do you think it would be important to talk with to continue my research?**

---

*IMPORTANT: Know that question <u>word-for-word</u>. Ask it verbatim; it is the most important question of the whole meeting. After asking the question, remain silent.

---

8. You will be tempted to talk if there is a moment of silence before the other person answers. Don't talk. Silence is your best friend here. Give the person enough time and respect so he or she can think it through. Take just a moment and give yourself 15 seconds of silence right now—I know, it feels a little uncomfortable. That silence is your friend… If they cannot come up with anyone to refer you to, be prepared to "prime the pump" for them.

9. Prior to any Informational Interview, come prepared with a list of 10-15 companies that you can have readily available to share with your interviewee (see Networking Brief). These companies will represent those within industries in which you want to work. The sole purpose of sharing this list is to help jog the memory of your interviewee in terms of identifying people at those organizations.

10. *Ask if it is OK to keep in touch by e-mail* (NOTE: Every 2-3 weeks you should be sending out a job search update to everyone you have met during your search. This update will be a summary of 4-5 bullet points of the people you met with recently, the names of organizations you are interested in learning more about, and a reminder that you are seeking referrals to people from those companies).

11. Thank the person for his or her time and promise to keep in touch. In addition, obtain the interviewee's business card so you have contact information going forward.

That's right, all of this is what you need to accomplish in 20 minutes. To put it in perspective, you need to gain the confidence of a complete stranger you've been referred to in just a half hour. That's not enough. In addition to the interviewee feeling confident about you, he or she must be WILLING to introduce you to other important people. These individuals could include friends, family members and colleagues.

Do you now understand why every part of your introduction and achievements are so important to have written, scripted and practiced? Your ability to connect with these influential people and show them you can solve problems, make someone's life easier and get them closer to reaching goals is the difference between either acquiring a by name referral and becoming just a person's way to pass time.

Please note that without direct name referrals, you have a limited number of people with whom you can meet during your search.

> *Using the HSE Process, if you get two direct referrals from each person you meet —you literally can never run out of people to assist you with your research. It's a mathematical certainty!*

What if I do not get a name referral from my meetings?

This takes us back to the conversation of WILLING and ABLE. There are only two possible reasons someone does not give you a direct name referral. They were either UNABLE or UNWILLING to do so. Immediately after a meeting where you did not receive any name referrals, it is very important to self-debrief and reconsider if the person was UNABLE or UNWILLING to provide such information.

If you do not take the time to follow along here step-by-step, you will keep repeating connection mistakes again and again. You need to adapt to the results of each meeting. Realistically, what are the chances that a business professional who has been in the industry for years doesn't know anyone you could talk to in his or her field? The chances are close to zero. So why didn't this person refer you to someone by name?

They were UNABLE. Sometimes jobseekers make the mistake of not clearly defining themselves and their skill set. Worse, they have regressed and presented themselves as someone who can do "anything for anyone in any circumstance" (that is why it is so important to follow HSE Process from the outset). If your message does not help these key people narrow down the connections in their "mental Rolodex," then you have made it impossible to narrow their choices based on your definition. The bottom line is they didn't know what you wanted.

They were UNWILLING. This is a slightly more complex problem. In this case, the person knew exactly what you wanted, but decided not to introduce you to his or her acquaintances. This was because the two of you did not establish a connection, or the other person could not fully understand the value that you could bring to an organization. Regardless of the reason, you need to adjust your presentation if you find yourself on this side of the fence regularly. People will rarely tell you that they are uncomfortable referring you to their friends.

This is why it is so important to practice your Informational Interviews with people from your ABC List. These people already know you well and will openly and objectively tell you the truth. As I often say, a real friend is the one who will tell you that you have a piece of spinach caught in your teeth.

Who will I be targeting to have these Informational Interviews or Networking Meetings?

Again, you first need to have four or five of these types of meetings with people from your 1000/1000 and "Who thinks you are awesome?" list before you hold them with someone you don't know well. The saying is, "Start easy, start close to home, but start today." If practice makes perfect, then I want you to make all of your mistakes with people who will give great feedback and are WILLING to help you.

Once you're comfortable from all of the practice, let's examine your target audience for these meetings.

> **Rule #1 in your HSE research project:**
>
> **If at any time in this process you are meeting with someone you don't already know or haven't been directly referred and introduced to, you are doing this WRONG.**

What do people really hate about the idea of networking? It is the FALSE idea that networking has to do with introducing yourself to random strangers from random organizations and then somehow a miracle will happen and it leads to the job of your dreams. That's the way it is shown on TV and in the movies, right?

But that never made sense to you, did it?

It is irrational to think that a series of conversations with strangers would lead to a miracle ending. I often refer to that as the "fairy tale" ending! But that is what "people" told you that networking was, and so you started down a path of cold calling on important people in the hope of stumbling on the connection that would change your life.

Let's be clear. That is not networking, that is begging. So what IS HSE networking?

Who you SHOULD be meeting during your research…

✓ Two people from your 1000/1000 list to explain the concept to and practice your presentation. You may get great referrals from these people that are incredibly WILLING to help you, but that isn't the goal.

✓ Choose the three people who are most WILLING to help you from your "Who thinks you're awesome?" list. It is important that you know and like them so well that calling them to meet is fun and exciting and not at all intimidating.

✓ Even if you get great referrals from your contacts, stick to your "Who thinks you're awesome?" list. It is Important that the first 5-6 of these meetings are comfortable and even fun. If you do this part right, not only should it not be scary, it should be like a family reunion!

What type of people are we hoping to get referred to?

These individuals should be one step above the level you would likely come into an organization. If you're a supervisor, your target will be someone like an operations manager. If you are a salesperson, then you'll want to meet with sales managers.

The rationale here is simple. You want to meet with people who have the problems you are well equipped to solve. If they understand how you can **"solve their problems, make life easier, and get them closer to meeting goals or bonuses,"** these people will see your value. They also hang out with other sales managers who have similar problems you could solve. Lastly, sales managers, for example, are most often responsible for hiring sales people.

If people network with others at their same level (project managers meets with project managers), you run the risk of being a threat to the person you're meeting with. ***It is very important to meet with people who are responsible for solving the problems you are uniquely qualified to solve.***

As discussed earlier, Networking Meetings are different than Informational Interviews. Networking Meetings are less about specific industry information and more about meeting with people who know others for a living. Examples of this demographic would be salespeople, pastors, public relations professionals, elected officials, educators and small business owners. Basically, I am referring to folks who work in a "people profession." These are people who "know people for a living" and understand networking VERY well.

The last idea I want to leave you with on the topic of networking is to include people who have been unemployed in the past few years and successfully found a new position. There is value in connecting with these individuals as well (I see it every day in my HSE Program because we have built such a strong community. Our "landers" keep in touch and help others!). What did they do to find their new position? Who did they meet with? How did they determine which companies or industries they should focus on? Did they utilize a strategically-planned form of job search or was their landing random? In a way, this Networking Meeting is also an Informational Interview, isn't it?

If the goal is to talk to people who "live in the world that you want to live in," then what could you learn from someone who has just gone through what you are experiencing? As I've said before the most common mistake people make in job search is they attempt to do it on their own. Without having these of discussions, aren't you destined to make the same mistakes others have made? Why not learn from their experiences?

Keep this saying in mind: "Unless you are inventing something, don't ever do anything for the first time. Find someone who has already done it and learn from their experiences." Let that one sink in for a moment. Don't let your ego get in the way here. ***Remember, people want to help you with your job search, but they don't know how. You need to teach them how to help.***

CHAPTER 12: NETWORKING MEETING SCRIPTS
How-to Conduct a Networking Meeting

1. Thank the person by NAME for meeting with you and give your **60-Second Introduction.**

2. Clearly state the goal of today's meeting and the best way for him or her to help you is by receiving a referral (or referrals), BY NAME, of people they think could talk to you about your search.

3. *Ask the person to tell you a little about him- or her- self.* Remind the person who referred you and why. Ask questions about how networking helped foster success in his or her career.

4. **Describe the type of organization you are ultimately hoping to work** *in* (size, industry, publicly held, family owned, etc., and any industries of interest).
   Now, ask the person, *"With the organizational description I just provided, can you list two or three organizations in our area that fit this industry?"* This helps ensure the idea of what you are looking for mirrors the image of what he or she is thinking about—in other words, it's so both of you are on the same page.

5. **Describe the type of role you want in terms of duties, responsibilities, authority and level.** Now, ask for an example of a job that comes to mind (it does NOT need to be an open job) that fits the description of what you hope to be doing in your next position.

6. **Give examples of achievements to validate your skill set is appropriate for the position you are seeking.** Watch for signs (verbal and nonverbal) from the other person that signify you will be a good fit for an organization.

7. Once any validation of your value or fit (for an organization) is demonstrated (again, verbally or nonverbally), ask specifically for BY NAME referrals. ***"I want to again thank you very much for meeting with me today. As I mentioned, I am networking with leaders in this area to do my job search. The best way for you to help me today is to provide a referral or two of someone who could help advance my research. If you were me (pause), who do you think it would be important for me to meet with in the next few days for advice, guidance and feedback?"***

8. Once you receive a referral (DON'T do this until you have received a referral), *ask if he or she would be WILLING to include you in any other emails in which you were being referred to someone else moving forward.* Then you can directly follow up with that referral. Again, this is a passive (yet important) alternative, so we don't want to focus on this step before exhausting the proactive way of receiving referrals (as opposed to you being referred on to someone else). Get the names when you can!

9. Ask if they have any additional advice about your job search before the two of you part.

10. Thank the person again for his or her time and promise to keep in touch. (and actually keep in touch).

Again, relevant networking is neither an art form nor an exact science. While you will likely develop your own string of questions after doing a number of networking meetings (and that is a good sign of progress), I advise you to start by using the above script as written. People new to networking usually are quite nervous, and therefore don't really drive the conversation in any measurable direction that helps them. Without a script, you will have a number of very nice conversations, but you will not receive any specific advice or BY NAME referrals. Without this type of information from the people with whom you are networking, how do you keep your search going in the right direction?

> **Example: A word-for-word Networking Meeting**

At this point it might be helpful for me to show you what a typical Networking Meeting looks like. I will use an example of my own from when I was connecting with people in colleges to teach the HSE Process. I met with a friend during my search and I had no idea how he would be ABLE to help me. All I knew was that he was WILLING.

Chris: Thank you so much for meeting with me, Jay! As you know, I am currently on a search to find organizations that I might be able to connect with for the purposes of teaching a new way of job search.

Jay: I'm happy to help, Chris, but as you know I'm not really connected to anyone in the teaching ranks so I'm not really sure how to help you.

Chris: Don't worry about that. The best way you can help me with my search is with a referral to anyone you know who lives in the world of education in any way shape or form.

Jay: OK. Maybe you could tell me a little more about what you do.

Chris: You and I have known each other for a long time but you really only know me as a football coach for a team you played on. While I love that part of my life, I spend most of my time teaching proactive job search at colleges. This is the type of job that I am looking for.

I have spent the last 5 years as a career advisor to hundreds of professional people, teaching them a whole new way to search for a job. The last two years, though, I have wanted to bring this process to colleges so it could be taught to students about to go on their very first job search. While I have had the opportunity to speak on this topic for a couple of local colleges, I would like to do it for colleges across the state.

Jay: Well, the only person I know is a friend of mine named Doug who I have known since childhood who happens to work in the athletics department at UW Madison. I've seen your work and heard you speak on job search and I think that he would be very interested to talk with you. I have no idea whether he will be ABLE to hire you, but he might be worth talking to as a way to start. Would that help?

Chris: WOW...That would be incredible! Don't worry about if he is ABLE to hire me to do work for the college. Any advice he could give me about how the UW system works would be really valuable. As I said, I am really just doing a research project right now about what might be valuable to state colleges. No matter what role he plays at the college he certainly knows more about the inner workings of it than I do. Would you be able to send him an email to introduce me and suggest that it might be good for us to meet?

Jay: That's no problem. Actually I've been thinking about calling him for a few weeks just to catch up and see how he is doing. This would be a great reason to do that.

Chris: That would be great. Please just email him and cc (carbon copy) me on the introduction email so that I can follow up from there. Jay, you have no idea how helpful you have been to me!

Jay: But remember, I have no idea if he is actually ABLE to bring you to campus or pay you anything.

Chris: That doesn't matter at all right now. If he isn't the person I ultimately need to talk to then he will at least be able to give me advice, guidance and feedback that will be invaluable to reaching my goal. Thank you so much! You have no idea how helpful you have been!

Was that effective? I am very proud to say that the result of my conversations with Doug ended up allowing me the opportunity to write the career search curriculum for UW Madison's Athletics Department and I have served as a guest instructor in their department for several years.

Remember, I had no idea where this referral would lead. All I knew was that I needed more information about career search instruction at a state college and talking to someone who "lived in the world that I wanted to live in next" was the best place to start my research.

CHAPTER 13: THE NETWORKING BRIEF

People only know you however they know you…

While you're in fine-tuning mode for these meetings, how will you actually put the scripts into action? Remember, in order to get hired you need to be talking to people in your industry. That means the only reason to network through HSE's Informational Interviews and Networking Meetings is to gain referrals to people in your industry to further your research and ultimately land a rewarding career.

Consider this process from the perspective of the people with whom you are about to meet. Whether you are about to meet someone you have known your entire life or someone you met as a result of a referral, the success of the meeting will be determined by your ability to "paint a picture."

The individual you are meeting must get a good sense of what kind of person you are, along with an understanding of the skills and achievements you can offer your next employer. He or she also needs to understand the type of organization you hope to work in. If the person is confused with any part of your presentation, he or she will be UNABLE to narrow down the "mental Rolodex" to give you BY NAME referrals.

This is a pretty easy concept to grasp if you are meeting with someone new. What most people miss in the HSE Process is that this is much more difficult if you are meeting with someone you have known a long time. While this may sound counterintuitive, think about how these people know you. Do they really know you based on your career path, your duties and work-related achievements, or do they know you because you have been social buddies on weekends for the past five years? They may know whether you like olives in your martini or tartar sauce with your fish on Friday night (Friday fish fries are a big Wisconsin thing). You have spent hundreds of hours with them, but what do they know about your work history, skills and achievements?

You need to make sure that the people who are WILLING to help you are ABLE to help you. Unless you help them understand who you are as a professional, they won't be able to assist you. This concept became very real to me when it happened during my own a job search.

> **Making someone WILLING to help you…ABLE to help you… (An example from the author's life)**

Scott is a terrific and compassionate school administrator in my geographical area. Every year during the past decade, both our families share a weeklong summer getaway in a small cottage in northern Wisconsin. With lots of people crammed into a two-bedroom cottage for a week, let's just say being friends is one thing, but seeing one another at 6 a.m. with tussled hair and in pajamas means you know them at a very different level.

During our annual "cottage" week, Scott and I also spend time together fishing. We discuss EVERYTHING. Children, marriage, finances, parents, and growing older are among the endless topics we discuss. There is no limit to the value we place on each other's advice. Let's just say we KNOW each other.

In 2008, I walked away from the paper industry to start teaching career search on a full-time basis. I had been doing it in one form or another since 2002, so Scott and I had talked about this over the years at the cottage. As you can imagine, his connections within local school systems could be very valuable to me as I started to contact high schools about speaking to students.

I thought that one conversation with my best and most WILLING friend would lead me to connecting with principals across the area, and with his referrals I would be "in like Flynn." When I casually asked Scott if he would connect me with regional administrators so I could tell them about my work, his response shocked me. "Why do you want to meet with them?" he asked. "What is it exactly that you do, and why do you need to talk to them?"

I was momentarily floored. My good friend was not opening up his mental Rolodex to me. Why? Wasn't I good enough? Wasn't I smart enough? Did he think I would embarrass him in front of his colleagues? Maybe he thought I lacked experience. All sorts of awful ideas traveled through my head. For just a moment I thought, "If he really was my friend, he would be falling all over himself to help me!"

Instead of becoming mad or shutting down, I decided to help Scott understand me in a different light. Subsequently, he and I talked in-depth about my work. The discussion included what I could bring of value to students. Suddenly, he opened up to helping me. As his knowledge of my professional situation grew, so did his WILLINGNESS to help me get in front of the right people.

We had a great conversation in which he not only gave me BY NAME referrals, but he helped me better understand how public schools operated and the best ways to contact people there. Wow, out of all those conversations in the boat while we were fishing that included work as a general topic, there was still enough lack of understanding between us to cause a real eye-opening moment for me... and hopefully for you.

From this story, remember two lessons:

1. *People only know you the way they know you. Don't assume anything.*

2. *People want to help you with your job search, but they don't know how; you need to teach them how.*

Enter... the Networking Brief

A Networking Brief is a document you will email to the person you are going to have an Informational Interview or Networking Meeting with about 48 hours BEFORE the meeting. The goal of the Networking Brief is to frame the conversation ahead of time so there is a certain expectation between the two of you before meeting in person.

The two of you can hit the ground running with a clear understanding of who you are, what you are looking for, your achievements and organizations of interest. Networking Briefs should be one page and email is the preferred method of submittal in case the person you are meeting wants to forward it for additional contact and networking purposes on your behalf.

The Networking Brief contains four main parts

1. **A summary of your job search objective** (this comes from your 60-Second Introduction)

2. **A list of achievements** which you have already created as part of the HSE Process that demonstrate you have the skills for success in your next career.

3. **A list of your technical and people (soft) skills** that will allow you to be successful in the job you seek.

4. **Organizations of interest.** This will help spur the person's memory of people they know. The list also serves as confirmation of the types of organizations you will describe to the interviewee.

The Networking Brief will be an evolving document as you learn more during your HSE research project. You will add and subtract organizations, change skills and achievements you choose to present per each unique opportunity, and so on. Your search objective will change a little, too, based on what you experience. Remember, this document isn't for you. It is for the people with whom you are about to meet.

Amazing things happen when you give people the opportunity to mentally prepare for these conversations. I often hear of HSE jobseekers who attend a meeting after they sent a Networking Brief and find that the other person already had names ready to share with them!

See the sample networking brief at the end of this workbook

Marketing Overview

1. Create your job search marketing pieces—Tagline, Focus Statement, 60-Second Intro, and Networking Brief.

2. Using the list of networking questions from the book, conduct your first Networking Meetings with people on your 1000/1000 List. These will be your first major interactions, so you will be nervous and unsure of the Process—that's why you are doing them with people who are incredibly WILLING to help you. Explain to these people that the meetings are practice runs for you, but that they can significantly help you with your job search by actively participating, providing feedback and referring you to other people to network with.

3. After your first meeting, ask the person what overall message was received during the dialogue. Was it clear to this person why you asked to talk? Does this person understand how to help you with your search (through information and referrals)? After you described the type of organization you were hoping to connect with, could he or she make a short list of organizations that fit that description? At the end of each of your networking meetings, ask your 1000/1000 List person to create an ABC list of their own detailing the names, position held and how he or she knows them. Ask them to send that list to you in a day or so, so you can identify which of the people on the list you would like to be connected to.

4. Now conduct 3-4 Networking Meetings with people "who think you are awesome." Focus on meeting with people like former co-workers, bosses, neighbors, mentors, etc. - those who already think positively about you.

5. Start conducting Networking Meetings with individuals on your B and C List... focus on people who are WILLING to help you first (even though you can't immediately identify whether they are ABLE to help you.) These will be either Informational Interviews (if you are talking to people in the target organizations or industry) or Networking Meetings with a focus on asking people you know to get you to people in your target industry. The focus is always ongoing research. Never ask anyone to "get you in" somewhere because that will turn them off very quickly.

6. Once you have completed 5-6 Networking Meetings and are starting to feel comfortable with the Process, set up meetings with people on your A List. Explain to them how you are going about your job search. These people will identify immediately because they would search for a new role the same way. Ask specifically for referrals to other A List people, including hiring managers and business owners. Ask them to evaluate your presentation and solicit constructive guidance on how your message came across. Ask them for feedback on your Networking Brief and to focus their referrals on your Target List of organizations.

7. The goal is to receive no less than two "by name" referrals from each person with whom you hold a Networking Meeting. You are talking with people who want to assist you; let them know the best way to help you is through introductions. At the end of the meeting when you ask for referrals, be sure to have your Networking Brief on the table in front of you to help this person identify organizations of interest.

8. As you begin meeting with people with whom you have been referred by your 1000/1000 and ABC Lists, be sure to approach them only after your contact has e-mailed or called to make the connection for you. Once that is done, send the person you were referred to a Networking Meeting request via email, and attach your Networking Brief (which makes it easy for these people to forward if they decide to). If the person doesn't respond to your request to meet, ask your connection (who referred you to them) to contact them and encourage a meeting with you. Again, the goal is two referrals from each person you meet with. Getting at least two makes it impossible for you to run out of people to meet before you land your next position.

9. Continue applying for posted jobs, but only apply for positions that truly fit. Spend only about 25% of your time responding to posted positions. For measuring your activity, use 20 hours per week as your target goal, not including any time applying for or researching posted jobs. Aim for 20 hours a week setting up and conducting Networking Meetings and Informational Interviews. Your target should be holding five meetings per week. Meet with three people each week you already know and two people each week you don't know, but have been directly referred to.

10. Evaluate weekly whether your activity is leading you closer to your goal. Are the conversations getting you closer to your target organizations or people? If not, it's time to refocus and recalibrate. Don't confuse activity with progress. Does it feel like your work is getting you closer to the people who have the problems you can solve for them? If you are not getting closer, do you need to redefine your message?

11. Identify and join a local job search support group. Share with others in the group how you are going about your search. Teach the HSE Process to another jobseeker as an introduction to something different. As you teach it to them, you will understand the process at a very different level.

12. Create a complete and professional LinkedIn profile. Begin connecting with people on your ABC List through LinkedIn. Review their connections for people you would like to connect with for Networking Meetings or Informational Interviews.

13. Track your activity and progress on a chart you review with our accountability person or group. Evaluate and adjust your activity based on progress toward the goal. (Use the activity tracker at the end of this workbook).

14. Limit non-value added activities like TV (two hours/day max.) Volunteer during each week to stay active and facilitate connections. Stay physically active.

15. Become active in community groups to facilitate connections. Avoid isolation at all costs.

16. If your search stalls, reconnect with former co-workers and 1000/1000 List people. Restart the process from scratch, if needed.

CHAPTER 14: TAKE ACTION
How to stay focused on the right things

The role of Accountability Groups

I am a huge fan of Accountability Groups. Everything I have experienced through developing the HSE Process suggests that the number one factor in moving your job search forward after the step-by-step instruction is joining or forming Accountability Group. This is a set of 3-5 HSE jobseekers who meet weekly to review their job search efforts, develop new ideas and leads for each other, and hold one other accountable for doing what needs to be done at 8 a.m. every day for the next seven days. The people in your group should come from different backgrounds and industries so there are new views of the world for you to explore. You should also only invite people into your Accountability Group who represent opinions that you respect.

There is no shame in being unemployed if you are working hard to solve that issue. Shame, however, is a great motivator if you have to report to people you respect and didn't do what you promised. The fear of looking people you trust and respect in the eye and telling them you didn't work hard on your job search is usually enough to get people to act.

The two greatest motivators in job search are shame and fear.

In these meetings you will not only share ideas and help each other on your searches, but you will also promise the group a certain level of activity that you need to report on the following week. In most cases, the fear and shame of disappointing the group is enough to overcome your hesitation in making connections and having the conversations with people you promised. Think of it as a pledge.

People in Accountability Groups need to be firm, but fair. The group's goal is never to punish inactivity with harsh words or guilt, but to investigate the core reasons for inaction and then provide support and solutions. The goal for everyone in the group is the same: to find their next great career opportunity. On any given day, your contribution to the group might result in a connection to help someone else, or it could take the shape of a compassionate ear to cushion the blow of a job interview that didn't end favorably.

Accountability Individuals

It is possible to have a single person be your Accountability Group, although I highly recommend going with two groups—one that is an individual you respect and the other is a group of 3-5 current jobseekers. The individual serves as more of a mentor or a coach, and the Accountability Group offers diverse perspectives, but both dynamics are similar in their essential functions.

Who you select as your accountability person is very important. There are three traits this person must have:

- ✓ **Employed and be free of any personal or professional crisis.**

- ✓ **An ability to assertively and objectively speak the truth to you. Sometimes the disclosures may be difficult to share, yet you know he or she will converse in a respectful and supportive way.**

- ✓ **Personal and professional opinions of you that matter to you.**

You must have a high opinion of your accountability individual. The idea of disappointing this person should make your skin crawl. You should be sweating bullets if you have to tell this person you didn't conduct the HSE activity you promised. These are important points. Without this type of relationship the person will be just another face for you to complain to about what you're going through. The individual's ability to motivate you comes without words because your respect for this person is that strong.

Who might qualify as your accountability individual?

1. A former boss or coach who was your mentor in the past.
2. A 1000/1000 List person who has shown the ability to lovingly kick your butt for good reason.
3. A leader for whom you have tremendous respect.
4. Your father-in-law or mother-in-law (your own father and mother might be too close to you to create the positive pressure you need).
5. A brother or sister who leads other people or business processes for a living.

It generally does not work well to have your spouse or significant other be your accountability person. These people care for you at the deepest level and may have the tendency to say, "Oh it's all right, you'll do better next time." There are moments in the HSE process where you need such doses of unconditional support and caring; this isn't one of those times.

Significant Others

A jobseeker's spouse or significant other can be valuable in the HSE Process. Let's look at how they might be feeling as you are going through this.

Job search is an emotional rollercoaster and your spouse or significant other will be on that rollercoaster with you. It is important to include them in your search. There is no one who has a more vested interest in your success; they will also be living through this with you on a day-to-day basis. They will want to help you in any way that they can, but will be unsure how.

Here are some guidelines on how to make them an integral part of your search and turn them into an advocate and an incredible resource for you.

Include your spouse or significant other from the very beginning. From the moment you learn you will be unemployed, let them know. This is not something to hide and it is not fair to do so.

Have them read this book with you and help you with the assignments. Use them as your first opportunity to test your Tagline, Focus Statement and 60-Second Introduction. Have them help you remember achievements that you might not have remembered.

Ask them to review your contact lists (1000/1000, "Who thinks you're awesome?" and ABC lists). They will remember people you have long forgotten or maybe just didn't come to mind. Have them make these three lists of their own contacts that might be helpful to you during your search.

Agree on an acceptable level of activity between the two of you. There is nothing more hurtful than one part of the partnership thinking the other one is not doing enough to solve the unemployment problem you SHARE. Agree on a certain number of hours you will spend on your search each week. Agree on the number of jobs you will apply for and the number of Informational Interviews and Networking Meetings you will hold each week.

Agree that once the jobseeker has met the agreed upon activity level that the rest of the time they can be doing something other than search for a job. Fill that time with family activities, working out or volunteer work. This will help take the emotion out of the conversations for both of you.

Ask your spouse or significant other to become actively involved in making connections for you. This will include giving them a clear understanding of the types of people you would like to talk to for your research based on industry and job type.

Meet at the end of each week to go over your meetings and research to discuss where you are in your search and where you are heading next with it.

Your spouse or significant other desperately wants to help you with your job search, but they don't know how. Another way of saying this is, "They are WILLING to help you with your search, but you need to teach them how to be ABLE to help with your search." Reading the book with you or during the process will help them a great deal. It will also prepare them in case they ever need to do a job search and your roles are reversed!

Acceptable Activity Level

Unlike most job search coaches, I do not believe you need to spend 40 hours a week on your job search. In fact, I think it is counterproductive. The common phrase is "finding a job is your full-time job!" That phrase usually has jobseekers looking at online job boards for 25 of those 40 hours. Not only is that not productive, but it shelters them from the only interactions that really matter during your search: *face-to-face interactions.* I cannot tell you how many jobseekers go into a deeper and deeper funk as the weeks pass because they are chained to their windowless basement office while looking online or changing three words every other day on their resume in order to generate responses. One thing is for sure, if confidence and focus sell during your job search interactions, then sitting in your basement for 25 hours a week sending emails to people you don't know in the hope that ANY of them will respond is the opposite not going to help you build confidence.

Stress in job search comes from feeling out of control. Sending out resumes to strangers you know will probably never respond to you just deepens your frustration and feelings of helplessness. Having other people judge you without ever meeting you and deciding your fate without even talking to you is maybe the most depressing thing you can do. But when people don't hear back from the resumes they submit, what do they do? They send out more resumes and the cycle continues and the emotional hole gets deeper. Just think. You are convinced resumes don't work after getting no responses, so you are going to do it more frequently and efficiently?

Isn't the definition of insanity doing the same things over and over but expecting s different result?

Here is what I consider an acceptable level of activity for the HSE Process:

You will work on your job search every week 20 hours per week. It will be broken out by <u>two hours per week</u> looking online for jobs and <u>three hours per week</u> applying for those jobs. <u>Two hours per week</u> will be spent attending job search support groups in your area or meeting with an Accountability Group. <u>Three hours per week</u> will be spent doing company research to identify targets for your search and learning about those organizations through online resources like Reference USA and Hoovers. <u>Five hours per week</u> should be spent identifying and connecting with people for Informational Interviews, Networking Meetings and sending out contact requests to them using LinkedIn or email connection responses. The last <u>five hours per week</u> should be used for actually holding your face-to-face job search meetings (Informational Interviews and Networking Meetings). That's your 20 hours!

After your initial assignments are complete you will hold 3-5 Informational Interviews or Networking Meetings each week.

Apply for three posted job ads each week using traditional job search methods (job boards and resume submissions).

After you have fulfilled your 20 hours per week, you should spend the other 20 hours of your normal work week volunteering, exercising and renewing old acquaintances. These activities will revitalize you and keep you from going into a downward spiral of emotion as you perform your search.

Years of experience with thousands of jobseekers prove this level of activity will create opportunities, and help you feel energized and fulfilled. Balance in your life is of the utmost importance during your job search. Staying in a positive mindset will keep you from settling for a second class opportunity and ensure you show up to every job search meeting excited and full of hope for all the world to see.

> **You will find a weekly activity log in the back pages of this workbook. Use it every week to track your activity level and commit to sharing the results each week with someone to create accountability for yourself.**

CHAPTER 15: OOPS!

Common Mistakes You Are About to Make

Activity vs. Progress (needed activity levels defined)

The level of activity you need to successfully use the HSE Process is easy to define, but remember that activity doesn't always equal results.

You must meet each week with three people who already know you (networking for job search introductions to people they know) and meet with two new people (met through referrals) you didn't know when the week started who can help you with your search.

The key to meeting with people, though, is to track progress, not just chart activity. If you are not meeting with people inside your industries of interest, and instead of meeting with a lot of random people, the referrals you receive will likely not bring you closer to talking with individuals who need you to solve their problems. Remember, each referral should bring you closer to talking with "people who live in the world that you want to live in" for your next job.

While you may start with people not in your industry or job type (your 1000/1000 List and ABC List), the goal is to receive referrals for people who are. If you're not attaining this goal, it's time to revisit your job search Focus Statement and make it clear to people who you would like to be introduced to.

Determining which ABC List people can help you before meeting

The most challenging jobseekers I work with are engineers, accountants and some information technology (IT) professionals. These are smart people, but their training has taught them to always think linearly to get from point A to point B. People like this tend to look at most things either as 'black or white.' This type of thinking leads them to evaluate the value of the people who they will be meeting before the conversation even takes place. Whether this happens prior to the meeting or at the outset of the dialogue, this is a HUGE mistake. The HSE Process is a research project and a constant quest for discovering information; therefore, IT IS WHAT YOU *THINK* YOU KNOW that will keep you from having the most valuable job search meetings.

Not meeting with your brother-in-law because you don't know exactly what he does for a living keeps you from the 500 people in his mental Rolodex. Not meeting with the leader of your religious organization because it is "too touchy/feely" for business keeps you from the 1000 people in his mental Rolodex. Not having this conversation with your spouse because you believe "if he or she could have helped me on my search, he or she would have done so already" makes the most significant and WILLING person in your life unable to help you.

Some of the most amazing HSE landing stories that I have witnessed started with the disclosure, "I wasn't even sure why we were meeting and what we were going to discuss, but I knew the other person was WILLING to help." People want to help you with your job search, but they don't know how. Continue to teach them that the best way they can help you is with a referral to others.

Trying to be Gumby

During your job search, you will naturally encounter some indecisive moments. Out of human nature, you will be tempted to mold yourself into being a viable candidate for positions you already know don't match your interests or qualifications. In HSE terms, we call this "trying to be Gumby." Out of frustration or not knowing what else to do, you try to convince hiring managers of organizations <u>you are something you are not</u> in order to end the pain of unemployment.

As the old saying goes, "when you are a hammer, everything looks like a nail." When you are unemployed and scared, every job looks like a good job. This is how people end up in careers that are a bad fit.

If you need to take a short-term job that isn't a great fit to keep food on the table and the lights on in your house, that is understandable. *But realize that this job is not your final destination*; it is simply buying you time to go through the entire HSE Process. You take this job to finance the rest of your search and your life.

Using HSE the wrong way (to obtain direct job interviews)

All too often jobseekers use this process as some trick to get in front of hiring managers so they present themselves as a potential employee. The HSE Process is not designed to place its jobseekers in front of hiring managers to pressure them to make a direct hiring decision.

Hiring managers understand the process I am trying to teach you better than you do. They likely used (or are familiar with) many parts of this process themselves and know how it is supposed to work. Trying to fool people into interviewing you by sneaking in the door under the disguise of a Networking Meeting tells them one thing about you. It reveals that you are willing to sacrifice your personal and professional integrity. How many of those types of people are hired under this approach?

Use the process correctly in front of hiring managers and you will typically hear, "You are going about this the right way." Use the process incorrectly by tricking your way inside an organization and you will more than likely hear the door closing.

Not keeping the pipeline full

Think of your job search as creating a wave of constant activity. If the biggest problems you have with your job search are that nobody knows you exist and you are unaware of at least 85% of organizations in your area, then solving those two problems will create a wave of activity.

That wave requires constant effort that lets people who are unaware of you know that you exist, are available and are talented.

That wave of constant activity has people talking about you and your search in emails, lunch conversations and next to water coolers.

That wave has hiring managers talking about you when they ask each other, "Who's available right now?" If you create enough conversations about your search, news of your availability will eventually reach the ears of the person that needs you to solve the problems in their organization.

Creating that wave requires dozens of conversations. To go from unknown to known in the minds of hiring managers takes a lot of effort. The average HSE jobseeker will have about 25 Informational Interviews or Networking Meetings before they land the role they set out to. (Some have landed with fewer, while others have taken longer, but this is a general average).

The hardest conversation I have with people is after a "sure thing" job opportunity falls through. They were so sure about a job offer that they stopped their networking activity. They let the wave crash. They say, "I don't know what to do next." I reply, "You know exactly what you need to do next. You just won't like the answer very much. Go refill the pipeline of people to talk to and recreate the wave of activity that you had two weeks ago."

They need to start from scratch, and that is more than all right to do. It just takes much longer and more effort to get restarted. Remember, until you have a job offer, you have nothing- keep the process going.

Poor or no tracking along the way and trying to fly solo

When is the last time you completed a project without planning the needed steps and tracking your progress against? If the boss from your last job gave you a project and you didn't give him or her an update, how did that conversation go?

Timelines exist in project management to hold people accountable to achieve specific goals by certain times. Some tasks need to be completed before other essential ones can even begin. Without tracking your progress toward established goals and a timeline, you are just taking random actions and hoping for a good result.

Again, commit to 20 hours a week with only two of those hours on the computer or applying for posted job ads. Meet with no less than five people per week, face-to-face. Three of these individuals you should already know and two will consist of referrals from others.

Create profiles of organizations that fit your career passion and research these companies in order to be able to approach them for referrals. Follow the networking meeting concepts and steps outlined and seek help from others while showing your value in solving workplace problems.

I challenge you to do each of these tactical steps as prescribed and not fly solo looking for random opportunities. Make your opportunities count instead of relying on a hole-in-one. Share your progress and timelines with to let them hold you accountable in a friendly and supportive way.

Expecting others to advance your search for you

Who is the person that is most motivated to solve your job search problem? YOU! Even though HSE jobseekers rely on people who are WILLING to help as part of the process, it is important to note that the only person who is totally committed to helping you find your next opportunity is you.

Think about your best friend in the entire world. This person is probably on your 1000/1000 List. You would do almost anything for one other. This is your go-to person when you have a difficult problem to solve or even address a sensitive family issue.

Now ask yourself these questions: How much time do you spend thinking about your best friend when you are not around this person? Do you wake up in the middle of the night worried about how this person's job is going? Do you have moments during the day when you worry about how your best friend will pay for his or her college tuition? The answer is probably no.

For better or worse, right or wrong, we are all too tied up in our own lives and families to spend any real time worrying about someone else, especially when we are not with them regularly. With this in mind, I want you to think about what happens if you ask the people who are WILLING to help you for assistance in your job search and then don't follow up to keep them engaged.

We have a tendency to believe that after we talk to people who are WILLING to help us with our job search they are "on assignment" for us 24/7. After all, aren't they actively making contacts for you when you are not around them? Aren't they dutifully scoping out job possibilities and making notes of companies they think you should contact along the way? Again, when even your best friend is not around, how much time do you spend worrying about what is going on in his or her life?

This is why it is important for you to consistently check in with these people (your 1000/1000 List, ABC List, and those who make up your Accountability Groups) to update them on your search.

"Out of sight, out of mind" is a phrase you should remember in this context. The only way these key contacts will be constantly on the lookout for possibilities (people or companies) is if you keep them updated on your progress. Meet with these people (your closest ABC List people, for starters) every two weeks over lunch (you buy), or send them email updates. Think of it as playing "reporter" by providing news updates on your job search!

Remember, if these individuals don't hear from you in several weeks, they may very well assume a talented person like you has already landed a position and not think about your search anymore. It is your job to keep the people who are WILLING to help you actively engaged for the duration of your search.

If your search stalls, are you UNWILLING or UNABLE to continue?

Almost predictably, your job search efforts will stall somewhere along the way. If you recall, you go through the Process steps that make up the Definition stage. Then you dig right into the RESEARCH stage as you become aware of organizations that you never knew existed. Even in the MARKETING stage, you will meet with people close to you with great fervor and anticipation. You will receive referrals and be referred to others, and your HSE job search will be on a roll. Then the wheels fall off.

Whether it is having trouble getting a response from someone you are trying to meet or hitting a brick wall getting in front of someone at the company of your dreams, you will find yourself at a point where you look in the mirror and say, "What do I do next?" Analyzing this question and breaking the answer into "UNWILLING or UNABLE" is the best way to get restarted.

When you are stuck during your search, find out if you really don't know what to do, or if you are just UNWILLING at the moment to do what needs to be done. Frustration with the job search process is different than not knowing what to do next.

If you truly have "hit the wall" in your job search, hold a couple of "sure thing" meetings. These are meetings with people with whom you have already met during your search and are incredibly WILLING to help you. Update them on your last five meetings (Networking or Informational Interviews). Let them review your recent research and ask for ideas. Describe to them what you have learned during this process along with what has surprised you.

You might want to have one of these meetings with your spouse or significant other. It always amazes me how underutilized these people are during job search. Who could be more motivated to help you during this time?

You may also be shocked that some of your spouse's connections can lead you to people to meet with as well. Everyone has a "mental Rolodex" of people who you don't know. Make sure to take the time to teach your significant other that connecting you with people is the best way he or she can help you.

If the answer to your question is that you are truly "UNABLE" to continue the process (genuinely don't know what to do next), then start again with the MARKETING phase. You may even need a refresher from the RESEARCH unit.

After you have learned from the Networking Meetings and Informational Interviews, what do you now see differently from your research? Present your research to someone else and ask this person to reach some conclusions for you based on what you have learned. Meet with your Accountability Individual or Group and review your conclusions with them.

In the MARKETING Phase of HSE, the task is to meet with people to discuss your search. It is not possible to "run out of people to talk to." In my hometown area, for example, there are more than 250,000 people who live here. When a jobseeker comes to me and says, "I've talked with everyone that I can," how do you think I respond? With just a little sarcasm, I reply, "Tell me about the first 500 people you met."

Usually when people think they are "UNABLE" to do anything more with their search, they really need to expand their view of who is available to potentially talk to and what is around in terms of organizations.

Can you imagine a salesperson coming back to his or her sales manager and saying, "There's no one left to sell to; I've talked to everyone." New ideas will not always come from your own perspective. You hit a brick wall because you've exhausted basically all of the possibilities from your perspective. Help others find new perspectives and new possibilities for you.

Disregarding PIPs (Previously Important People)

These people are defined as people who have held important and connected jobs during their work life but have retired. Now in their retirement years, these people value simpler things like freedom, experiences and sharing all of their hard-earned knowledge. What many people miss is that they still have all of the industry knowledge and contacts they did when they were working. But now they just have more time and desire to share it! Unfortunately, with all that knowledge to give, very few people are willing to ask for their advice, guidance and feedback. As HSE jobseekers, though, we know better. We know that their experiences and connections are critical to our success.

Not only do these people have great life experiences to draw from, but they also remain deeply connected to their community through volunteer and philanthropic work. The people that they knew—AND STILL KNOW—may be the exact type of person you need to talk to.

Learn about the nationwide organization, SCORE (Service Corps. of Retired Executives). The organization has local chapters and nationwide online options, and the group's sole purpose is to make available the wisdom and experience of retired executives to the next generation. The organization has lists of people for you to choose from who have had virtually every experience possible in the work world! It is an incredible idea. If we don't ask for advice from people who were faced with similar problems at one time, we are destined to make all of the mistakes they did. Why not learn from their experiences?

Retired people have performed job searches and can give great guidance on how they did so successfully. How did they go about it? With whom did they meet? What would these people do today if they had to do a search on their own? It is true for all people—ask for their advice and they will talk all day. In the case of PIPS, retired individuals actually have time for you when they're not out making the world a better place by helping others.

Relationships don't end when someone retires. It just takes on a different form. In this more advanced form of relational networking, retired people can easily meet with their connections and ask if they would be WILLING to meet with you.

News Flash: These people aren't PREVIOUSLY important people at all. They are vibrant, CURRENTLY important people who have the flexibility in their schedules to get involved in your search (If you can prove to them why you are worth helping, (hint, hint) go about it as the HSE Process has scripted).

Trading imperfect action for perfect inaction

The last mistake you are about to make in your search is not doing anything until your presentation or choice of person to meet is EXACTLY right. I call that perfect inaction.

In doing the primary HSE steps (Definition, Research, and Marketing), you will have ample opportunity to improve your Focus Statement or do additional research. People can fall into the trap of spending dozens of hours perfecting their 60-Second Introduction without ever getting in front of anyone to actually deliver it to. They can spend 100 hours or more on researching organizations that might have the problems they can solve, yet never actually approach any of them.

If anything, understand this: To land your next job, you need to talk to someone face-to-face at some point. Even when jobseekers send resumes, their ultimate goal is to ask for a job interview. HSE is all about creating those face-to-face conversations from a different angle, but the goal is the same: talking to people. The more time you spend perfecting your message, the less time you actually deliver that message to someone who can help you.

Let's be clear. I want you to spend enough time doing each one of the HSE steps that you are well prepared to meet with people; don't shortchange that. On the other hand, you can also see that sitting in your basement changing three words in an objective instead of meeting with someone could be easier. I have a word for that and it's called HIDING.

The greatest human fear is not being important to anyone or anything. The second greatest fear is being judged by others. I fully understand why people primp and preen their presentations to the point that they never hold a meeting. They are scared. That is the entire reason for starting with people you know and who are incredibly WILLING to help you.

I promise you will make mistakes with your first Networking Meetings. That's why you hold them with people who like and believe in you already. If you make a mistake, so what? You don't have to be perfect for them to help you. Make your mistakes during these practice runs so that by the time you are meeting with people you don't know, your presentation is polished and confident. You will be better the third time you have a Networking Meeting than you were the first time… and the fifth will be better than the third. Then anything can happen!

Don't worry about meeting with the exact right person. Meet with someone! Don't deliver the perfect message. Deliver a message! The hardest part of any project is getting started. Always choose imperfect action over perfect inaction. There is no perfect action… just action that gets you closer to your next great career opportunity.

The interesting part of having guided hundreds of people through this process is that I cannot only predict how your job search will go, but I can forecast the mistakes you will likely make. It's only human nature that people, given a highly-structured and predictable process, try to circumvent it. These mistakes can most often be characterized as mistakes of ego. At the same time, these mistakes may be your best ally along the journey.

HSE can help you understand this whole ego-driven mistake factor. Remember: most people believe they can find their next position alone and without help. When I tell you that you need to be humble, sincere and ask for help, throw away your belief that asking for help is for weak people. As you can see through the HSE Process, the only thing weak about asking for help is not asking at all.

If you get stuck during your HSE journey, go home…

This is the last piece of advice I will share. Remember that there will be high and low points during your search. One moment you will be sure you are meeting the person who desperately needs you and the next you will be frustrated that no one will return your calls or agree to meet with you. If you get to a frustrating point in your search, go home.

Going home in this case means going to meet with people close to you who are WILLING to meet for you to gain perspective and get back to a positive mindset. Going back to your 1000/1000 list will guarantee a positive interaction that will restore your confidence and a sense of hope. If you have a meeting that doesn't go well, schedule your next meeting immediately with someone from your "Awesome" list to make sure that bad taste in your mouth from the last meeting doesn't last.

Going home means refocusing all your efforts on people who are WILLING to help you. When in doubt, go home.

There you have it! You now have the power to land the job you desire and deserve!

One last piece of advice when it comes to who to start your HSE networking with at the very beginning of your HSE job search research project.

Once your preparation is done and you are ready to have your first networking meeting…the question of who to have your first meeting with comes up for every new HSE job seeker. The simple answer is to identify people who are most WILLING and most ABLE to help you. We do this by creating a Conversation Value Index **(CVI)** number for each person on your contact lists. Here's how it works:

For every name on all of your lists (1000/1000, ABC and "Who thinks you're awesome" assign a value of 1-5 (5 being high, 1 being low) for each person as to their WILLINGNESS and their ABILITY to help you on your search.

For example: Your mom might be very WILLING to meet with you about your search (WILLING-5) but she knows nothing about your industry (ABLE-1). Her combined CVI is 6.

The boss from the job you just left knows all about the industry (ABLE-5) but he is the one that let you go (WILLING-1). His combined CVI is also 6.

But your good friend (WILLING-5) is a consultant in the industry you are looking to get into and knows all the people and organizations in the industry (ABLE-5). His combined CVI is 10 and would be a great place for you to do an initial informational interview with.

Remember, start easy, start close to home, but start today. Now let's get to work!

Postlude: A plumber's journey: Your Human Search Engine model landing story from start to finish.

This story illustrates how the entire HSE Process of Definition, Research and Marketing works in the real world (and will work for you).

Imagine a plumber moves to a new town and is looking to generate business. He knows very few people other than friends who are not in the plumbing industry.

His first business generating effort is to create a wonderful marketing piece to mail to all homeowners in town. To ensure he doesn't "miss any opportunities" (sound familiar in your job search?), he makes this print piece as generic as possible. He indicates on his marketing piece that he can do "anything for anyone" and no job is too big or too small. He takes great pains to indicate every one of his areas of plumbing expertise on the brochure and assures people that he has the lowest prices in town with 24-hour-a-day service.

The plumber prints beautiful brochures (just like your resume) and distributes them to every house in town. Any home or apartment building that has plumbing is blanketed with his brochure. After distributing the brochures, he waits by the phone just knowing that soon it will be ringing off the hook.

Predictably, no one calls. (How often do you respond to junk mail that is randomly sent to your house?). The plumber is frustrated. He not only doesn't generate much interest, but he sees his brochures thrown out or recycled all over town (Does this sound familiar with your carefully-worded resumes ending up in the "no" pile?).

Out of frustration, our plumber decides to attend a home show. Clearly people at a home show are there for a reason and can likely be expected to have an interest in plumbing services. Just like you would promote yourself during a traditional job search, the plumber continues to do anything for anyone. New homes, old homes, geothermal heating systems, sink and toilet replacements… he can do it all. Surely now that he has cast a wide net over this group of people who have a similar interest in home building or remodeling (or they wouldn't have come to the home show), he should now have people demanding his service.

The plumber does receive some calls after the show, but they are all for competitive pricing quotes. Subsequently, he only acquires a few of those jobs. Most often he finds that the jobs are going to more established plumbers in town who are being recommended to customers. The plumber is not being evaluated on his expertise or problem solving, but only on his pricing. Worse yet, because he has advertised that he can do any type of plumbing work, his prices are compared to EVERY type of plumber and handy man out there!

Out of sheer frustration, the plumber visits one of the few people in town he knows and explains the problem to this person. This person asks the plumber, "What makes you unique enough for a stranger to want to hire you even when they have established existing plumbers to choose from?" The question struck him harshly; he hadn't really thought about it like that before. As the question became clearer to the plumber, it occurred to him that the people with plumbing jobs choose who to hire the same way that he has bought almost everything in his own life... through a referral from someone known and trusted.

Given the opportunity to choose a stranger or someone whom they know and trust, people will almost always go with what and who they know. People crave certainty, especially when talking about the biggest investment in their life... their home. The plumber's shoulders sagged as he started to think that there is no way a stranger can compete with existing plumbers in town.

A friend of the plumber asked him, "What do you specialize in?" He replied, "Well, I can do anything in the plumbing industry!" His friend furrows his brow and replies, "So you really don't have a specialty; you are just like every other plumber in town. No wonder people are evaluating you just on price... there is nothing unique about you."

After contemplating a bit, the plumber said, "Well, what I really do better than any plumber than I've ever met is replace corroded piping in old houses." "Now we're getting somewhere!" exclaims his friend. "Now we can start to get you in front of people who have the problems you are uniquely able to solve."

The plumber's friend suggests he completely redo all of his marketing materials to primarily focus on repairing piping on older houses. While afraid that he will be marketing to too narrow of an audience, he understands his "shotgun" approach didn't work. He spends some time defining a specific target audience for his message (**Definition stage**).

Next, the plumber's friend takes him and his newly targeted brochures to a meeting of the town's historical society. He thinks to himself, "What a waste of time... there are no plumbing jobs to be found there." While he sits in on the meeting, the plumber realizes that everyone there has a unique knowledge of the older, historic parts of the city, including the historic houses in the city. He also learns there is a community group that meets once a month that consists of people who own historic properties in the city. These people either own or deal directly with the owners of these properties. His friend introduces him to that group.

While fighting off the urge to ask if any of them needed work done on their homes or if they know of anyone who does, the plumber just asked questions of the group and learned everything he can about this historical properties group. In the course of this conversation, his friend (who is there to give him credibility as a good person and as a good plumber) suggests that he should be invited to the historical property group's next meeting as a guest.

At that meeting, the plumber begins to ask the property owners about what unique problems exist with owning and maintaining older buildings. He begins to understand their issues and problems, and he doesn't try to promote himself as a solution because that's not why he came to the meeting. The plumber came to gain knowledge from people who "live in the world he wants to live in," the world of historic home owners.

He learns a great deal about specific problems they face, including trying to upgrade homes to today's codes, the struggle of replacing lead pipe with something that will not corrode and the balance of updating while keeping the historical value of the house, etc. (**Research phase**).

As the meeting continued, eventually someone asked the plumber specifically what he did for a living. Instead of saying, "I am a plumber who can fix any plumbing problem for anyone in any type of building," he simply provides a well-practiced statement: "I have been a plumber for more than 10 years, but really love to be involved with the refurbishing of the plumbing in older homes. Making these historic residences useable on a daily basis for people to live in really makes me happy." He smiles because this is no "sales line" to get their attention. It is a real explanation of his greatest joy in the world of plumbing.

The conversation quickly shifts to the plumber's experiences fixing the problems the group had just laid out for him. He discusses his jobs related to historical houses in the town he just came from. He tells these stories with enthusiasm because doing this type of plumbing really does bring him joy.

The plumber is then asked by the group to present a portfolio of work photos. His work in older homes gives him credibility. His friend speaks up and says that he is a really great plumber because he has done work for him as well. The group of historic property owners now sees the plumber differently because he has credibility from his portfolio and third-party confirmation from someone they trust (**Marketing phase**).

Without much hesitation, one of the owners of the historic homes asked the plumber about a plumbing problem at her older home. At first she asked for advice, but eventually *she asked him* if he would be willing to come over and look at the problem (He couldn't push his way in; he had to be invited). The others say that if this job goes well, they would be happy to have him assess their properties as well.

Over the next month the plumber becomes the "go-to person" for the historic homeowners. People are calling him for his advice and guidance and making him the default choice for the work on their homes. Not only that, but historic homeowners start to refer this plumber to people who have much newer homes, but still need plumbing work.

People made their decision to hire the plumber based on the referrals of others … not on his price alone. How did he get here? A friend led him through the HSE Process. No miracles, no accidents… just a logical, sequential series of events executed to create a desired outcome.

AUTHOR BIO

Chris Czarnik is a national career search expert with 12 years of job search counseling and motivational speaking experience. His innovative approach to job search has helped thousands of people land rewarding careers.

Chris currently serves as the Director of Student Employment Services for Wisconsin's largest two-year technical college, and is a leading adjunct career search instructor for the 5th largest research university in the nation. Chris' process, The Human Search Engine, was introduced to the 113th United States Congress as a national job search and workforce development model.

As a thought-leader in the field of career search, Chris delivers his dynamic presentations to groups of hundreds of people, as well as providing classroom and one-on-one instruction. His second book, The Human Search Engine – A Serious Jobseekers Guide, was released in January 2015.

To contact Chris for speaking engagements, book orders or to inquire about his upcoming Certification Program:

Email: info@careerresearchgroup.com

Website: www.myhumansearchengine.com

You can also find Chris at:

Twitter: @HSEChrisCzarnik

LinkedIn: www.linkedin.com/career-research-group

www.linkedin.com/ChrisCzarnik

Blog: www.careerresearchgroup.com/blog

APPENDIX

Sample Networking Brief- Experienced Job seeker

JOHN SMITH, CPA, MBA
1313 MOCKINGBIRD LANE, APPLETON, WI 54915
PHONE: (920) 555-1212 • E-MAIL: JOHNSMITH@YAHOO.COM
URL: www.linkedin.com/in/johnsmith

Search Objective:

Chief Financial Officer or Controller position in a small to medium company to manage the accounting function to provide accurate, complete, and timely financial data with comprehensive analysis necessary for making sound business decisions and achieving performance goals.

Background and experience:

5 years – Senior Vice President & Chief Financial Officer – Choice Bank
10+ years – Vice President Finance (CFO) – Oshkosh Savings Bank
8+ years teaching college level accounting, finance, and general business

Skill set:

Bachelor of Science, Accounting	Masters of Business Administration
Certified Public Accountant (CPA)	SEC reporting
Start-up bank	Financial analysis
Budgeting and long-range planning	Capital campaigns
Bank regulatory reporting	Manage accounting team
Freelance writer	Teach accounting to non-accountants

Achievements:

Experienced Chief Financial Officer (CFO). Accounting and analytical skills readily transferable to any industry. A "hands-on" leader who prepared a 3--year financial business plan to earn charter for start-up bank in Oshkosh. Did all record-keeping and provided assistance for shareholders in start-up bank to raise a Wisconsin record of $21.6 million in capital and start bank that has grown. Served as CFO to help bank grow to $120 million in assets in three years and achieved profitability in third year. Successfully completed all Securities & Exchange Commission (SEC) and bank regulatory reporting for start-up bank.

Companies of interest:

Kimberly Clark	Hewlett-Packard Company
PepsiCo	Microsoft
BMO Harris	Chase
General Electric	AIG
Boeing	

Sample networking brief-New college graduate

Elly Smith

5931 Elmwood Lane, Anywhere, WI 54915

PHONE: 920-555-1212– EMAIL: esmith@gmail.com

Search Objective:

A program coordinator position involving creating, implementing and improving programs to help marginalized populations for a non-profit organization whose mission is to improve the lives of children and people with disabilities.

Background and experience:

8 months – Volunteer event coordinator Special Olympics

3 years – College Admissions Student Worker, 1 year as Student Coordinator

4 years – Counselor, YMCA Camp proceeded by 7 years as a volunteer

4 years –Women's Soccer team, 1 year as Captain

Skill set:

Bachelor of Arts, Political Science   Lifelong experience with people with disabilities

Leadership and coordination   Organizing and motivating a group of people

Writing and editing

Achievements:

Experienced success in academics and extracurricular activities while graduating cum laude. Spent 7 years as a volunteer at YMCA Camp leading to employment as a Camp Counselor. Successful employee of the College Admissions Office, was promoted to Student Coordinator. Qualified for National Tournaments in both Soccer and Mock Trial.

Companies of interest:

YMCA

Boys and Girls Club

Big Brother Big Sister

Habitat for Humanity

Sample Informational Interview Request Email

To: Simons@yahoo.com
From: smith@gmail.com

Subject: Referral from Tina Wilson

Dear Mr. Simons:

Tina Wilson suggested I contact you because of your expertise in the area of banking and finance systems. I am on a career search and would value your insight and experience in the field of banking in the Milwaukee area.

Please understand that I do not expect you to have nor know of opportunities at this time. I am going about my career search in a way that I believe will produce better results than conventional methods.

I have been involved in all aspects of finance for the last 7 years, but my passion is in the area of large real estate transactions where I utilize my leadership, analytical and problem solving abilities. The leadership and solutions I bring to a team make a difference in the implementation of lean banking initiatives. This work has increased the organization's level of internal quality systems and improved the loan approval process while reducing their overall costs. I want to continue in this direction and pursue a position in the banking and finance sector in the greater Milwaukee area.

I would like a brief meeting with you to discuss banking and the need for lean practices in a finance setting. I will also be asking for some advice and feedback.

Please feel free to reply to this email with times that fit your schedule. I will come prepared and very much look forward to meeting you. I understand you are busy, and promise to be brief.

Sincerely,

John Smith

Sample HSE Blended Resume

JOHN SMITH
1313 Mockingbird Lane
Anywhere, WI 54915
jsmith@yahoo.com

PROFESSIONAL OBJECTIVE

An Information Systems Coordinator position in a progressive firm utilizing proven skills in analyzing, training written and verbal communication, and problem solving, to assist a growing organization enhance its customer service while maximizing revenues and growth in the industry.

SELECTED ACHIEVEMENTS

- ANALYZED problems with the design system. Troubleshot software for bugs and held vendors accountable for bug fixes and tested software after installation; implemented written procedures to get personnel trained on the new software. **Results:** Improved designer's performance and quality on the new software.
- COORDINATED the installation and training of new design software; created curriculum and training programs. **Results:** Reduced learning curve by 20% and increased productivity for all designers by 30%, reduced time to market.
- DEVELOPED & COORDINATED an Access database program for the creation and tracking engineering change orders. Eliminated outdated paper creation of change orders; eliminated manual filing; directed IS personnel to implement the changes to the system. **Results:** Reduced man-hours spent in engineering change order system by 30% and increased accuracy and accountability by 40%.

WORK EXPERIENCE AND KEY ACCOMPLISHMENTS

Vandelay Industries, Anywhere, WI   **2012 to Present**

Electrical Designer/Coordinator/Warranty Administrator

Responsible for documentation of the electrical department, coordinating projects, and warranty claims.

- **Designed** Electrical Systems for Fire Trucks Using CAD System.
- **Created** Access Database for shop orders and special purchase orders.
- **Coordinated** projects between manufacturing, engineering, and sales department.
- **Created** and updated design files.
- **Investigated** warranty claims for fire trucks and equipment.

Smythe Corporation, Anywhere, WI   **2005 to 2012**

Printed Circuit Board Designer

Responsible for designing printed circuit boards to meet customer requirements and project deadlines.

- **Designed** high-speed printed circuit boards, surface mount, and multi-layer, double-sided and single-sided PCBs with controlled impedance, matched lengths, and routed differential pairs.
- **Created** and revised procedures to increase productivity.
- **Developed** a relationship with vendors to ensure on-time delivery.
- **Maintained** relationships with customers to ensure 100% customer satisfaction.

EDUCATION

B.S. in Business/Management

Upper Iowa University

Graduated Magna cum laude

A.S. in Printed Circuit Board Design

General Studies Technical College

Dean's Honor Roll

TECHNICAL SKILLS

Advanced user of Microsoft products including: Word, Excel, PowerPoint, and Outlook.

Advanced database design and development skills with MS Access having designed databases to handle Bill of Materials, Purchasing Requests, and Engineering Change Orders.

Sample HSE Cover Letter

John Smith
1313 Mockingbird Lane
Appleton, WI 54915

Manufacturing First Co.
1212 First Ave.
Anywhere, WI 54915

Dear Hiring Manager:

In response to your advertisement in the National <u>Business Employment Weekly</u>, for "Operations Manager," please consider the following:

YOUR REQUIREMENTS	MY QUALIFICATIONS
Set and make happen aggressive monthly shipping plan	Over eight years aggressive program/production management experience; PLANNED, SCHEDULED, COORDINATED, EXPEDITED 100+ electronic defense contracts, meeting monthly fab, test Q.C., shipping schedules to include stateside/offshore subcontracting.
Bring continuous stream of new products from engineering release to production inventory ready to ship	Over 8 years of aggressive COORDINATED/INTEGRATED engineering configuration manufacturing new/prototype & existing designs from release to production – stock – delivery in multi–project environment.
Plan and implement a cost reduction program that has major influence on the company's performance	IMPLEMENTED/MONITORED earned value system; recovered $1M loss; INITIATED economies – of – scale production; increased 2% loss to 10% profit for business segment.
Maintain the company's reputation for providing quality products	INTEGRATED/MONITORED engineering, manufacturing, quality activities; CONDUCTED CCB reviews; won follow – on contracts.

Enclosed is my resume for consideration.

Sincerely,

John Smith

RESOURCES FOR RESEARCH

Hoover's, Inc., an American business research company that provides information on companies and industries.

www.hoovers.com

Reference USA, a national database for business reference and research. Requires membership (access) from a subscribing library.

www.referenceusa.com

LinkedIn, a professional social networking site designed specifically for the business community. Allows users to network and connect based on their position title, industry, company, professional interests, etc.

www.linkedin.com

State Manufacturing and Service Guide, a directory of manufacturers and business services published state-by-state. Available online (search YOUR STATE + Manufacturing and Service Guide) or through your local library.

O*Net a government sponsored and created job resource guide for looking up different jobs available in different industries. Details of each job includes, duties, responsibilities, education needed and salary information

www.onetonline.org

Personality Type Indicators, free, online personality assessment tools that may promote greater self-awareness to help job seekers define and achieve their goals.

www.16personalities.com

www.personalitypage.com

CONVERSATION TRACKER

The HSE process is about taking charge of your job search through activity <u>you</u> can control. Use the Conversation Tracker to keep a record your networking meetings. Your goal should be 3-5 completed forms (informational interviews) each week!

Name	
Meeting Request Sent	
Meeting Date/Time	
Meeting Location	
Meeting Notes	
Referrals	
Thank You Sent	

Download a PDF version of this worksheet at www.myhumansearchengine.com.

WEEKLY ACTIVITY LOG

How are you spending your days? **Not all job search activity is created equal.** Monitor your time to ensure your job search activity is productive and on track. Record everything from networking meetings to online research to volunteering to exercise. Show your Weekly Activity Log to your accountability partner(s) and discuss areas for improvement.

	Sunday	Monday	Tuesday	Wednesday	Thursday	Friday	Saturday
6:00am							
7:00am							
8:00am							
9:00am							
10:00am							
11:00am							
12:00pm							
1:00pm							
2:00pm							
3:00pm							
4:00pm							
5:00pm							
6:00pm							
7:00pm							
8:00pm							
9:00pm							
10:00pm							

Weekly Time and Activity Goals for Job Search

Searching for jobs online	2 hours
Applying for jobs online	3 hours
Attending job search support groups Meeting with accountability partner(s)	2 hours
Completing company research	3 hours
Identifying new people to connect with Sending contact requests, setting up appointments	5 hours
Conducting informational interviews/networking meetings	5 hours
Time Dedicated to Job Search	**20 hours**

Check off each box as you complete it.

Informational Interviews	1	2	3	4	5	Posted Jobs Applied To	1	2	3

Your goal is to hold 3-5 informational interviews and apply to 3 posted job ads each week.

Download a PDF version of this worksheet at www.myhumansearchengine.com.